TRENTSIDE MEMORIES

COMPILED BY SUE AND JON OLIVER AND THE TRENTSIDE LINKS COMMITTEE WHO ARE EMMA BARRATT, RICHARD FARLEY, DIANE KEYTE AND ELIZABETH ROSE. WE WOULD LIKE TO THANK THE FOLLOWING PEOPLE WHO MADE THE PRODUCTION OF THIS BOOK POSSIBLE:

MARGARET ADCOCK, CLARE ANYAN, RITA ATKIN, MEL BANHAM, SHARRON BANHAM, ANDREW BARBER, RICHARD BARNARD, GLADYS BAYES, JEAN BERNHARDT, GILL BLOW, DR DAVID BOSTWICK, ALISON BROWNLOW, RODGER BROWNLOW, JOHN BURKE, ROSEMARY BURKE, SHIRLEY BURY, BARBARA BUTLER, DEBBIE CANNING-JONES, IAN CLARK, JANETTE CLARK, STEVE CLAYTON, JOYCE CUPIT, SUSANNAH DICKINSON, THE LATE FRED DIXON, KERIS EYTON-WILLIAMS, SUSAN EYTON-WILLIAMS, MONICA FARLEY, DAVID FENWICK, THE LATE IAN GOURLEY, PAT HAMMOND, ALAN HARDWICK, WALTER HAVERCROFT, ELISE HAWKER, RANDAL HAYES, MR & MRS HEWIN, JUDE HIRST, CHRIS HEWIS, DOUGLAS HOGG, SARAH HOGG, DAVID INGLEBY, STUART KINCH, DORIS KITCHINSON, COLIN KYME, GILL KYME, SUZANNE LANGFORD, SARAH LIDGETT, TREVOR LOCK, DENISE LOCKWOOD, JOHN MANNION, JOHN MATTHEWS, CHRIS MEDLEY, BRUCE MINNITT, SANDRA MOODY, MR & MRS A MORRIS, RALPH NEEDHAM, LORAINE OLSEN, LYNN PETERS, MARK PETERS, JIM PORTER, THE LATE MALCOLM PORTER, PAT PORTER, PAUL PUMFREY, JOHN REDGROVE, YVONNE REDGROVE, SHEILA REDSHAW, SUE RICKETTS, KATHRYN ROBINSON, LORAINE RONTREE, JON SASS, MARGARET SCOTT, JOAN SCHIPKE, PHIL SIMON, GILL SNOWDEN, PETER SNOWDEN, MIKE SPENCER, RACHEL STOW, JIM TOWNEND, COLIN WATSON, HANNAH WATSON, ALISON WELLS, DON WEAVER, TERRY WESTON, MAGGIE WHITING, RICHARD WHITING, ANN WHITWORTH, BERNARD WHITWORTH, DAVID WILLEY, MR & MRS G WORRELL, KENNETH WORRALL, TERRY WORRALL

PREFACE

In 2009 we took over a community magazine, during the following years we saw it grow, covering 14 villages and hamlets and reaching 1600 homes and businesses. We were keen to learn the history of these villages as very little seemed to be documented. We were delighted by the generous spirit of the parishioners and received lots of information and photos. We felt we would like to share this with our community and so sought a National Lottery Heritage Grant to enable us to produce a book. This book is not a serious historical record but rather a general outline of each village/hamlet together with a middle history that we can relate to bearing names and photos from the past.

CONTENTS

The Dickinson family, 1903
(full image & caption page 17)

BRAMPTON

Brampton is a hamlet in the West Lindsey district of Lincolnshire, which lies approximately nine miles north-west from Lincoln and just under a mile north-east from Torksey village. The parish of Torksey historically contains the three ancient townships of Brampton, Hardwick and Torksey, with the early 13th century parish church of St Peter, Torksey being at the centre of local rural life for centuries.

Introduction

The first known documentary reference to Brampton appears in the Domesday Book of 1086, when it is referred to as Brantune, a hamlet of just five households: four villagers and one freeman. The area had 40 acres of meadow and 10 of woodland and the manor had recently been acquired by the Bishop of Lincoln from the Abbey of St Mary, Stow.

Few records survive from the early days of Brampton. The manor was still in the possession of the Bishop of Lincoln when Oliver of Sutton was enthroned at Lincoln Cathedral in 1280. During his Bishopric an account of the charters and title deeds for episcopal estates and their respective locations within the cathedral treasury was compiled. The oldest Stow Manor documents are contained in a bound volume of seventeenth century court rolls, and Bishop Oliver's account was copied into the front of this volume. The court rolls indicate, however, that the manor had passed out of ecclesiastical ownership; it was now the possession of the Rt. Hon. William Willoughby, Lord Willoughby of Parham in Suffolk, who in 1672 mortgaged the manor to raise funds for the marriage portion of his daughter, the lady Anne Willoughby (b.1652). The Willoughbys had owned land in Lincolnshire since the reign of Richard I. Lord Willoughby's main estate was in Hertfordshire and his last years were spent as governor of Barbados, but following his death there, his body was brought to Lincolnshire for burial with his ancestors.

Brampton's characteristically rural character has been retained throughout the centuries with a scatter of farmsteads historically providing the area's main economy with arable farmland predominating and,

later, a mix of dairy and arable. Towards the end of the 18th century, however, there was a major change in rural life with the Parliamentary Act of Enclosure of 1778.

The Domesday Book entry for Brampton, 1086. [Source- Open Domesday]

This agricultural enclosure altered the look of the landscape as the open field system of small unfenced strips of land scattered throughout the parish was transformed with the introduction of a new planned landscape with just a handful of landowners who leased their land to tenant farmers. This resulted in the loss of a swathe of common land and heralded the beginning of just a few farms providing employment. Unfortunately the map showing how Brampton lands were divided has not survived, although a copy of the accompanying apportionment which describes the lands and ownership is held at Lincolnshire Record Office. The principle landowners within Brampton following Enclosure were Annie Maria Amcotts and Frances Buckworth (sisters of the late lord of the manor Charles Amcotts Esq.), the Prebendary of Stowe Benjamin Laughton who received allotments of land in lieu of the parish tithes, Wharton Amcotts, George Booth, Amy Cole, Richard Cole, James Ellis, John Levett, Mary Laughton, John Millner, John Tallant, Henry Tallant, William Tallant and the Overseers of the Poor, whose

Extract from John Speed's Theatre of the Empire of Great Britaine, first published 1611_12. Brampton appears as 'Bramton.'

allotment was probably used to support Brampton's impoverished parishioners. As well as enclosing land, the Act also staked out the three main public roads or highways through the parish, the Turnpike Road, the Gainsborough Road and the Torksey Road, each of these set at forty feet in breadth. Similarly a number of private roads are described, and these, along with the fences that enclosed their lands, were to be maintained by the allottees. Thus the economy, geography and infrastructure of the parish were forever altered.

By the end of the 18th century there emerged a new phase of building in Brampton, reflecting a wider nationwide trend in rural areas, whereby old village farmhouses were subdivided into cottages and new buildings were erected. In Brampton this was seen in the building of Manor Farmhouse, Priory Cottage and The Beeches, with Hermitage House being built slightly later in the early 19th century. Freeholders built good quality houses as building standards became more accessible, and houses were constructed in 'polite' architectural styles usually in brick. Although bricks were taxed from 1784 they were a favoured building material, especially as improved transportation methods had made them more accessible.

By the turn of the 20th century Brampton had changed little and remained largely undeveloped with the exception of the establishment of a golf club to the south west. The scattering of small farms were gradually subsumed by Manor Farm to the north, which became the dominant landholding in Brampton, and several of the former farmhouses became private residences.

Brampton today remains rural in character, with a number of fine private residences, which were once at the core of its farming economy.

VILLAGE TALES

Brampton Potteries

William Billingsley moved from his decorating establishment at Mansfield, some seven miles east of Pinxton, in or shortly after June 1802 and established a small porcelain factory at Brampton. This was sometimes described as the Torksey Factory, but Brampton Manufactory was the original title and this name occurs in some rare marks or inscriptions. Although Billingsley undoubtedly supplied the knowhow, he needed backers to supply the funds in order to establish the factory. Mr CL Exley in his book The Pinxton China Factory (privately published by Mr & Mrs R Coke-Steel, Sutton-on-the-Hill, 1963) states that Henry Bankes, a partner in the Pinxton concern, broke a covenant by supplying funds to enable Billingsley to start the new Brampton China Works. Bankes remained a partner with John Coke of Pinxton up to 1st January 1803. The London

Gazette of 9 August 1803 records a 'Commission of Bankruptcy' awarded against Henry Bankes of Lincoln, Maltster, China Manufacturer & Dealer. However, the Dissolution of Partnership notice, as published in the London Gazette of 5 April 1808, lists the following partners in Sharpe & Company:

- ▶ William Sharpe
  Late of the City of Lincoln but now of Louth
  Plumber and Glazier
- ▶ Samuel Walker
  Of Brampton, Manufactory China Man
- ▶ James Walker
  Of Fillingham, Farmer
- ▶ Benjamin Booth
  Of Gainsburgh, Printer
- ▶ William Billingsley
  Of Brampton Manufactory, China Manufacturer

This very mixed partnership was dissolved on 15 July 1807 and the concern was then continued 'in the name of Samuel Walker' until at least 21st November 1807. It is not clear for how long the Brampton Manufactory continued after this; I think it then closed, or lingered on for a very short time until July 1808 when both William Billingsley and Samuel Walker left for Wales. The factory site was visited by William O'Neill in 1895, the report of which is printed in the Report and Papers read at the Meeting of the Architectural Societies of the Counties of Lincoln/Nottingham during the year 1895.

Extracts from this paper are reproduced below:

Being anxious to know if there were still any remains of Billingsley's kilns or factory in existence, I made a journey of exploration to Torksey on the 17th of June and two subsequent ones in July.

I discovered no traces of a factory of any kind in Torksey village. On hearing of my search, Mr South (one of the oldest inhabitants), pointed to a house on the top of a distant hill and said, "That is Pottery House and the farm of sixty acres attached to it is called Pottery House Farm". I then remembered that Billingsley in 1805 described himself as William Billingsley of Brampton, in the Parish of Torksey. The factory then, was not in the village of Torksey as most people thought, but at least three-quarters of a mile from the hamlet of Brampton, which consists of about a dozen houses.

A northwest view of the Brampton in Torksey China Manufactory

The pottery factory stands on a low hill about four hundred yards to the west of the Gainsborough road. Not far from the west end of the house the grass field is very uneven, with low mounds. Here I think the kilns were placed, and here also, the rubbish may have been thrown and piled in heaps. Doubtless, if these mounds were dug into, they would disclose samples of the various kinds of pottery and porcelain made in the factory.

A Torksey-ware Durham Ox Jug given to Mr Benjamin Wilmot of Newton on Trent from the Brampton potteries. The jug was given for non-payment of goods and is exhibited in the Usher Gallery, Lindum Road, Lincoln.

A few months ago in the course of conversation with a lady in her 88th year, she mentioned tea and coffee services of Torksey china in her possession which she inherited from her father (Mr Boot) who died in Lincoln in 1835. Miss Boot informed me that her father, wishing to assist Mr Billingsley who had just started a pottery at Brampton in the Parish of Torksey, employed him to decorate the services which were in a plain white state, but she does not remember having heard her father say whether he had first bought the china from Mr Billingsley or had the services previously in his possession. The china is highly gilt and the paintings, which are in medallions, are well executed. The paintings are all landscapes and are done in reddish brown monochrome, and the name of each view is written on the bottom of the piece. A sugar basin has on its front the 'Brampton Pottery House' painted, and on the back a picture of Torksey village and the old castle.

The majority of the paintings are views in Derbyshire and Nottinghamshire. The mark on the ware is two daggers in blue, meeting at the points. This tea service is of French porcelain, as are pieces to be subsequently mentioned, but Mr O'Neill also referred to other interesting pieces: a jug which is a very fine example of Torksey-ware and belongs to Mr Benjamin Wilmot, of Manchester. Mr Wilmot inherited the jug from his grandfather, whose initials B. W. are placed on the front of the vessel. Mr Benjamin Wilmot, in the days of the Brampton pottery, was a farmer and butcher, living at Newton-by-Trent, a village not far from Torksey, and supplied Mr Billingsley with meat. On one occasion when a debt was contracted by the potter, and the butcher had sent in his bill, the proprietor of the potteries presented him with the jug instead of cash! This jug can be seen in the Usher Art Gallery in Lincoln, where the fine and comprehensive Exley Collection is displayed.

Mr Coke-Steel went on to say:

"When I read this account, it seemed most unfortunate that William O'Neill had not taken the opportunity of digging into these mounds for the 'samples' he presumed were hidden therein. I therefore resolved that if I was ever in the neighbourhood, I would visit the site to see if by chance the mounds or factory wasters were still undisturbed. The chance was taken while returning from a holiday in August 1966. The farmhouse, once part of the Brampton Manufactory, was still standing in its solitary position. Many fragments of pottery are to be found in the garden and fields surrounding the farmhouse; these appear to date from the middle of the nineteenth century onwards and are pieces of domestic pottery discarded by the various tenants.

"The field mentioned by Mr O'Neill over 70 years ago does not now show the intriguing 'low mounds', but August is not the best month for tracing rubbish dumped over 150 years previously, as the growth of grass is so lush that it covers all but the most pronounced object. Within half-an-hour my wife and I found evidence to suggest most strongly that porcelain was made as well as decorated at the small Brampton factory. Apart from these fragments showing that porcelain was made at Brampton, existing pieces show that porcelains made elsewhere were also decorated there."

Hermitage House

The History of Hermitage House

Unsurprisingly, the history of Hermitage House is closely linked with Brampton's rural and agricultural history. Despite a lack of cartographic and associated documentary evidence showing land ownership in Brampton in the 18th and 19th centuries, a study of the Enclosure Award of 1778, selected land tax records 1795-1830, genealogy data, and census records beginning in 1841 and every ten years subsequently until 1911, has allowed a line of occupancy to be established. Thereafter, electoral registers and genealogy records have been utilised. A number of publications were also consulted, including newspapers and street directories.

According to an eighteenth century map, possibly drawn up around the time of the enclosure acts, the property where Hermitage House now stands was owned by James Ellis. However, land tax records suggest that the property passed into the hands of the Booth family.

The Owners of Hermitage House

Ownership of the house and associated land had remained in the hands of the Booth family throughout the 19th century, passing down to George William Sikes, the head of the household at Hermitage House. It was at this time that the house first appears with a name within archival records. From this date and indeed until the mid-late 20th

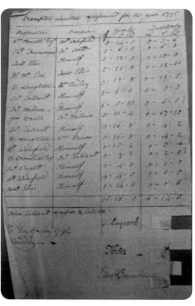

Land tax return from 1795 showing the land leased from George Booth to John Millner for £3 lls 4d annually

century it was known as The Hermitage, and the farm was thereafter known as Hermitage Farm.

The Denby Family

The Hermitage and Hermitage Farm were purchased from George Sikes by Jacob Denby (b. 1861) a farmer from Yorkshire. He was born in Baildon, Yorkshire, to parents Thomas and Mary Denby, who were respectively from Baildon and Bingley, Yorkshire. Thomas was a smallholder, farming 14 acres at the time of Jacob's birth. Unusually, Thomas was aged 50

Annie Sikes and her husband Ernest

Annie Sikes in later years

 Frontage of Hermitage House

and Mary 38 when Jacob was born, although Thomas' marriage to Mary appears to have been his second.

The family had moved to Bank Top Farm, Baildon by 1871, and Thomas' granddaughter Mary Hudson (b. 1867) aged four, was living with them. They had a young servant, Charles Hornley who was aged 14 at this time. Within ten years the family had moved again and were living at Butler Houses, Baildon, where Thomas was farmer of 50 acres. Another granddaughter, Alice Brook (b. 1875) had moved to live with them by 1881.

Jacob married Sarah Greenwood (b. 1858) early in 1882 in Keighley, Yorkshire. Sarah was from Bingley and they spent the first years of their married life in the tiny village of Eldwick, just outside there, where they had their two eldest children Mary (b. 1883) and Thomas (b. 1884). They returned to Baildon where they had a further six children, John Henry (b. 1885), William F. (b. 1886), Charles (b. 1888), Annie Florence (b. 1892), and twins Alice and Emily (b. 1897). By 1901 Jacob was working with his sons Thomas and William on the family farm, while John was working as a wool apprentice.

Jacob and Sarah moved to The Hermitage with their youngest children. Mary and John remained in Baildon and by 1911 were sharing a house at 13 Moorland Avenue. John had been promoted to a manager of a wool warehouse and Mary was his housekeeper. Thomas remained a farmer and is thought to have married and moved to nearby Sturton, where he lived until his death in 1942.

As the Sikes family before them, Jacob Denby and his family appear to have been very much part of local life; Alice Denby is known to have played the church organ at Torksey for church services, and they were seemingly highly regarded within the community. Life was not without sadness, however, as Annie Denby died aged 17 in December 1908 and was buried on Boxing Day, then just over a year later her younger

sister Emily died on 31 January 1910 aged 13; her funeral at Torksey church was said to have been well attended.

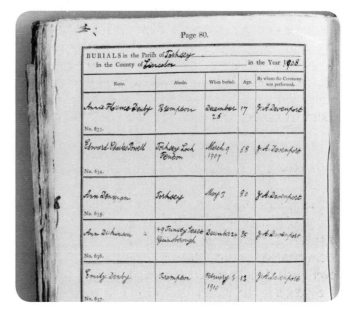

 Burial register entries for sisters Annie (top) and Emily Denby (5th), 1908 and 1910.jpg

In 1911 Jacob and Sarah were living at The Hermitage with their sons William and Charles who worked on the farm, and their only surviving daughter Alice, then aged 14. The Denbys employed a wagoner, Stephen Palmer aged 26 and a domestic servant, Gertie Higgs aged 16.

It was during the Denby's tenure that the first description of the property in any detail is recorded. In 1910 the government's Valuation Office undertook a nationwide survey of all lands and property in England and Wales for tax purposes. The survey for Brampton includes notes made by the surveyors relating to The Hermitage and Hermitage Farm, which are marked on an associated map.

The farm at this time encompassed 168 acres, with a gross value of £169 15s. The buildings including the house are described as being in fair to good condition and are listed as a brick and tile house, barn, cowsheds, stables, open shed and yard and cart shed, and a wooden shed. Although most of the farm was freehold 35 acres were still copyhold to the Manor of Stow, here called Stowe Court Manor.

The Denbys lived at The Hermitage and ran Hermitage Farm until 1940, although as expected, there were some family events during this time. Marriage indexes for the district indicate that both Alice and Charles were married by 1930, although further details are as yet unclear. Their brother William died in December 1922 aged just 36, and as many former occupants of The Hermitage before him, was buried at Torksey parish church. Sarah Denby died on 4 February 1939, aged 81, leaving Jacob a widower. Her funeral was also held at Torksey church, where she was buried.

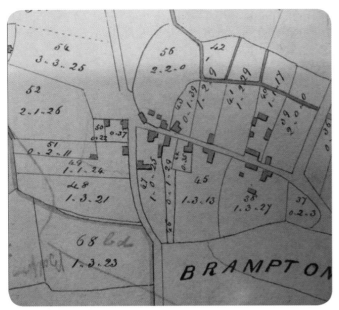

Extract from Plan of the Townships of Gate Burton, Marton, Brampton and Torksey in the County of Lincoln, 1843. The orientation of the original plan was rotated roughly 90 degrees clockwise. Hermitage House appears as an L-shaped building towards the centre of the image. The buildings depicted on the map may not be to scale, as the map was drawn up to show drainage within the area, rather than being for accurate mapping purposes.

In the following year Jacob Denby sold The Hermitage and Hermitage Farm to Charles Norman Dickinson and moved to Metheringham, possibly to live with one of his sons. However, his place of death soon afterwards, on 21 April 1941 aged 80, is recorded as being Prospect House Farm, Gate Burton. He was buried at Torksey parish church. He left effects of £7633 to his sons Charles, who had remained a farmer, and John who had progressed to being a wool merchant.

The Lee Family

Although The Hermitage and Hermitage Farm were purchased by Charles Norman Dickinson, the house was seemingly rented to tenants, whilst the farm was run by the Dickinson family who also owned and managed the adjacent Manor Farm.

The Hermitage was rented by Laurence and Elizabeth Lee. Laurence Cecil Lee was born in Gainsborough on 17 February 1915, the younger of two children born to parents Florence Elizabeth (1885-1963) and George (1876-1971), a law clerk. His older sister Constance Viola was born in 1907. The family lived in a house in Alfred Street, Gainsborough where Laurence was probably born. They later moved to Brampton, and George, Elizabeth and Laurence were living at Brampton Lodge in the years preceding Laurence's wedding to Elizabeth Joyce Marshall (1914-2006) in late 1938.

The newlyweds moved into The Hermitage during the Second World War. Compiling of the electoral registers was put on hold during the war years so the exact date of their arrival is unknown. Laurence served in the RAF Voluntary Reserve forces from 5 May 1942 and, whilst away, Elizabeth's mother, also Elizabeth, lived at The Hermitage. The Lees are known to have had two children, but their dates of birth are uncertain.

The Dickinson Family

Following the Lees' departure, the house was probably unoccupied for the next two years. Certainly no one who was registered to vote was at the property during those years. However, by 1950 it seems that Charles Dickinson may have moved into the house. His wife Kathleen, father Frank and son Michael were living at neighbouring Manor Farm, but Charles isn't listed there with them. His address is given in the electoral register simply as Brampton, and he may have been minding the Hermitage property until another tenant could be found. In the end he didn't have to look far. In June 1952 Michael Dickinson married Heather Lidgett in Lincoln, and the couple set up home at The Hermitage.

Michael was born in September 1930 in the Gainsborough district to parents Kathleen Latimer (née Hyland, 1903-1983) and Charles Norman Dickinson (1898-1961). Originally from Bradford, Yorkshire, Charles' father Frank (1859 –1934) had lived in and run Manor Farm since 1899, and it had passed to Charles and Kathleen. They had married in Pudsey, West Yorkshire on 2 June 1926 before returning to Lincolnshire where they raised their family.

Jacob Denby's sale of The Hermitage and Hermitage Farm to Charles Dickinson back in 1940 may not have been just for practical reasons; the two families were actually related. The wife of Frank Dickinson, Susannah (née Hardy) was a cousin of Jacob's wife, Sarah. It may therefore not just be coincidence that Jacob and Sarah Denby moved to The Hermitage from Yorkshire, in the year following the Dickinson's move to Brampton.

Charles Dickinson died at Manor Farm in August 1961. He left effects of £2242 which were granted by probate to his widow Kathleen on 20 February 1962. She remained at Manor Farm with her son Robert (b. 1932) and daughter Margaret (b. 1939) until 1964 when she and her son Michael's family made a swap. The eldest Dickinson son took his father's place at the main farm, while Kathleen and her younger son took on The Hermitage. Initially Margaret Dickinson lived there too, but it seems she married in 1966 and moved to Lincoln.

Kathleen and Robert Dickinson shared Hermitage House until her death in 1983. Robert Dickinson was there alone the following year, but the house was subsequently sold and the Dickinson's long association with the property came to an end, though

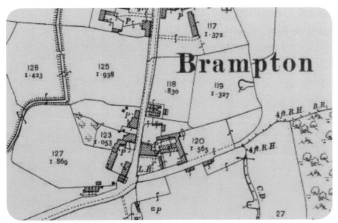

Extract from the Ordnance Survey Map of 1899, showing Hermitage House and associated farm buildings. The farm buildings had been added to since the map of 1843, with those to the east having a dairy function. The three cottages mentioned in the auction sale advert can be seen to the north of the farm buildings.

the family remained at Manor Farm until the 1990s.

The Coakley Family
For just two years in the mid-1980s The Hermitage was home to Peter R & Hilary A Coakley and Hilary's daughter Stephanie Saxton.

Hilary Annette Auty was born on the Wirral in the summer of 1940, the daughter of Harold Auty and his wife Phyllis Evans. Hilary had married John Saxton in Huddersfield in 1959, and they were the parents of three girls, Tarnya, Stephanie (born 1961) and Victoria. Then in 1978 Hilary Saxton married Peter Radcliffe Coakley. It seems Peter had also been married before, to Dorothy Millhouse. The couple tied the knot in his hometown of Scunthorpe in 1963. He had been born there in 1939 and was the son of John Radcliffe Coakley and his wife Frances Alice Peel.

After living in Brampton, it seems the Coakleys went to Harrogate where they ran a company called Osborne Fabrications Ltd. They later retired to Porthmadog. Stephanie Saxton is a hairdresser in Huddersfield.

The Townend Family
By 1988 The Hermitage, or Hermitage House as it had become named, was owned by James and Hilary Townend. In March 1995 they sold land adjacent to the house to Stephen and Susan Pope, although they retained access rights, when required, for maintenance of the gable walls of the outbuildings adjoining Hermitage House, and the roof and eastern wall of a garage which had been constructed on retained land.

Hermitage House has since been home to the Townends, thus continuing a two hundred year history of Hermitage House being a family home in the heart of Brampton.

MY STORY

Sheila Redshaw
(née Cumberlidge)

1935 - It was my fifth birthday when we moved from Heapham to Brampton. For my birthday I was given a brand new penny and a jam tart.

Dad was a wheelwright and joiner by trade. He worked for Mr Jacob Denby who lived at Hermitage House. I can remember going to pay the rent on Saturdays to the Hermitage where I would be ushered through dark rooms to see old Mrs Denby. She always wore a lot of jewellery and was very nice to me and gave me a penny each time I went - that seemed a lot of money to give a small child.

When Mr and Mrs Denby died, Mr Charles Dickinson

Sheila's father, George William Cumberlidge

13

Sheila & her 21st birthday cake

became our landlord. The Dickinsons were living at The Beeches and then went on to live at the Manor House.

I had a brother Winston, a sister Joan and a younger brother Marcus. Unfortunately, Marcus was born brain damaged. War or no war, there was no help or support from anyone in those days. He never went to school, he could walk but not talk. I was the one who stayed away from school to look after him if Mother and Dad were out, as he had a fascination to poke the fire. In my small way, I tried to teach him to talk and write.

In those days grownups seemed to speak in whispers if children were around. They said "Little pots have big ears". Even when Edward VIII abdicated and war broke out, it was always the same whisper; whisper and I knew something serious was going on.

Winston, Joan and I went to Torksey School until one of the teachers started to make Winston and Joan use their right hand, as they were both left-handed. There were many rows between Dad and the school and Winston developed a stammer, so we all went

to Marton School two miles away. As I was small I couldn't walk all the way, so Winston used to piggy back me until I was stronger. He was a good brother. We went in all weathers, rain, frost, fog and snow sometimes two to three inches deep, we had to go. We wore old socks

Zilpha Cumberlidge, Sheila's mother

over our shoes, no waterproof clothing in those days. No wonder we suffered with chilblains and the sniffles. We were happy there; the headmaster and his wife were good to us. If the weather was really bad and we had wet clothes, we were invited into the schoolhouse for a meal. On Shrove Tuesday, the headmaster gave all the children a huge orange and the afternoon off which was a real treat. My brother left the school at 14 years-of-age.

Joan passed what is now the 11 plus, but could not afford the High School in Gainsborough. When Joan left Marton School, I was transferred back to Torksey as it was considered too lonely to go on my own. Also, by this time there were different teachers, mine being a Miss Rose Talbot, she and her sister lived at the Priory opposite to the Manor House in Brampton. Miss Violet Talbot taught the boys woodwork, the girls were never taught cookery - maybe it was because there was a war on. We had evacuees from Leeds with their teachers. A curtain was put down the middle of the big classroom - we were on one side, they were on the other. It did not last long as they were no safer here than in Leeds with all the airfields around. Some of the girls were really well dressed with their red jumpers and gymslips - I always wished I could have a red jumper and gymslip but it was not to be. Food rationing came in buff-coloured ration books for adults, a different colour for children. Adults' rations per week, per person, were 8oz of sugar, 2oz of butter and lard, 4oz of margarine and one egg. In addition, dried egg in a waxed carton - one allowed per family each month and 1oz of tea per person per month. We had to queue, especially if we went to Gainsborough to the butcher's, fish and fruit stalls. Tinned goods, soap, candles, clothing, shoes, materials, towels, bedding and knitting wool were on points and furniture was scarce.

As we had a very big garden we enjoyed lots of fruit

and vegetables, Dad grew raspberries, gooseberries, strawberries and rhubarb. Also there were two big Bramley apple trees, if there was a good crop, Dad would clamp them in the garden, for those who don't know what that means, it's what they did with potatoes to keep them over the winter. Dig a deep trench, line it with straw, put the apples or potatoes in, cover with more straw on the top and then a lot of earth to keep the rain and frost away, that way they would keep until the springtime. Of course it depended how many you used and it wasn't wise to open the clamps up if it was frosty. Nowadays, potatoes are kept in specially ventilated sheds.

Dad also grew lots of flowers - polyanthus was one of his favourites, people came from miles around to buy plants and he also had a cold frame and glass house. He also tried to grow mushrooms. We kept honeybees but never had any honey! Dad had permission to catch rabbits on the golf course and he kept ferrets in the pigsty. Rabbit meat helped out with the meat ration and the skins were sold to the rag and bone man.

Times were very different then.

Susannah Dickinson

A beautiful photo of the Dickinson family at home in Brampton

My grandparents Frank and Susannah Dickinson moved to Manor Farm Brampton from Yorkshire in about 1901, Jacob and Sarah Denby also moved from Yorkshire to Hermitage Farm about the same time, Sarah and Susannah were cousins.

I was born in 1939, the youngest of Charles and Kathleen Dickinson's seven children. The same as all the family I went to Torksey School, at first my sister

Ruth would take me on the back of her bike until one day I got my foot in the wheel and we both ended up in the hedge bottom - I had to walk after that!

Brampton was a busy place with horses, pigs, a few sheep and chickens, even Muscovy ducks and

Charles Dickinson, Susannah's father

An aerial view of the Dickinson farm buildings, note the haystacks to the back of the buildings

well looked after by trades people visiting from shops in the area. Mr Jubb from Saxilby even carried paraffin on his van. Others included Mr Lucas from Sturton, Jim Porter from Marton, Mr Addison the butcher from Fenton who used to arrive in the village about 9pm on a Friday evening, and many more.

As far as I know Ted Richardson was the first person in the village to have a television which he bought for the Coronation in 1953. After watching the Coronation we walked to Torksey where the locals had arranged a party in the schoolroom there.

Digging potatoes at the family farm in Brampton 1944

geese, also home to the very well-known Torksey herd of Pedigree British Friesians. The crops grown included potatoes, carrots, wheat, barley, oats, sugar beet and kale grown for cattle feed. The village had about 25 houses, all but four or five of these occupied by people who worked on the farms.

It was a proud day for Brampton when Ruth Dickinson married Alfred Rose in June 1949, lots of people came to watch - the whole village was decorated with flags and bunting.

Even though the village never had a shop we were

Manor Farm Brampton 1944

Brampton was fortunate to have electricity before the war, a lot of places in Lincolnshire were much later into the 1950s.

Brampton was a happy place to live in and many of us have very fond memories of our time growing up in the village.

 Mike Dickinson taking his new bull for a walk 1988 or 1989

Manor Farm Brampton 1940s, from the left: Frank Dickinson, Susan Bradbury and Annie Dixon

Walter Havercroft

Walter first moved to Brampton in 1945 aged 10. He lived in an end terraced house, now known as Bailey House, for almost 50 years. When he first moved there the three adjoined houses had all been recently renovated and extended to add a bathroom, kitchen and living area to the existing buildings. In the spring of 1945 a chestnut tree was planted to the rear of the property which is still there today with a preservation order on it. Living next door to Walter and his family were two ladies, Esme and Nellie Richardson. Esme was a post lady and her sister Nellie worked at the Dickinson's home as a housekeeper.

 The last haystacks in Brampton before the arrival of the combine harvester

Walter's father, William, worked on the Dickinson's farm with the horses and five years later William joined him. Walter remained here for all his working life and under three different employers, Mr C.N. Dickinson, then his son Michael Dickinson and finally when the farm was sold, for a Mr Whitton from Kexby for whom he worked his last seven years. Walter recalls doing many different jobs on the farm which was a mixed arable and dairy farm when owned by the Dickinson family. Walter has many memories of his time on the farm including Italian and German prisoners of war

who worked on the farm. After the war Lincoln prison used to send 20 of its prisoners to work at the farm which Walter thought was very exciting! They were accompanied by a warden and brought meat pies for their dinner which were warmed by the housekeeper.

 *Mr CN Dickinson, farm owner and Walter's employer*

Walter has now settled in Newton on Trent but looks back on his time in Brampton with warmth and a affection.

 Walter, in 1993 enjoying the Brampton BBQ

BRAMPTON IN PICTURES

This lovely Edwardian wedding photograph was taken outside the clubhouse at Lincoln Golf Club, in the village of Brampton in about 1908. The bride is Ella Earl and it is thought that the bride and groom left for Canada soon after the wedding. Those on the back row (left to right) are: Lister, Mary Toule (née Denby), Lang Toule, Alice Denby, unknown, Alma Hughes, Harry Dickinson and unknown. The middle row consists of: Charlie Denby, H Williamson, Charlie Hughes (Pop), and Ashley. Front row: Lister, Lucy Earl, Grannie Earl, Archie Earl, Kitty Earl, and Willy Denby. Seated on the grass next to the bride is Frank Hughes. On the other side, next to the groom, is Raney Hughes (later Burnett).

The marriage of Mary Dickinson and Tom Denby at Manor Farm Brampton. The photo is believed to be from the early 20th Century

Dan & Fanny Drakes, previous residents of Brampton

Main Street Brampton with The Hermitage on right and Beech House on left

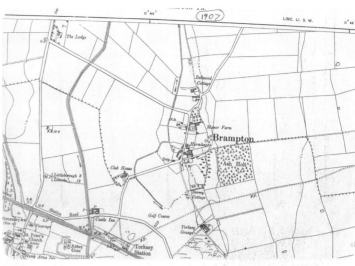

Amy Purchase (née Bramhill). Brampton resident, member of the WI and Brown Owl of Marton's Brownie pack. Amy was also a supporter of the Royal British Legion and collected tirelessly for their cause for over 40 years.

Brampton map 1907

A group of golfers outside Lincoln Golf Club, Brampton, in the 1920s

The Dickinson family: From left back row, Annie (later Arden), Harry, Sally (Sarah) later Park, Polly (Mary) later Denby, David. Front row Frank and Susannah Dickinson, Charles and Frances Susannah (Queenie)

Brampton Village pre -1945

DRINSEY NOOK & PARK FARM

Introduction

D rinsey Nook is a very small hamlet located at the junction between the A156 and A57 roads, about eight miles from Lincoln. It was originally an island before the neighbouring land was drained, 'Nook' describing the slight projection of dry land among meadows subject to flooding. In the absence of earlier spellings one can only guess at the meaning of Drinsey, which could have been formed from the Old English 'Drenges ege', meaning 'Dreng's island'.

Despite being a place that most people pass through in their cars en route to the A1 or Gainsborough there are tales to be told about Drinsey Nook, and some of them are very dark indeed.

20

VILLAGE TALES

Plane Crash at Park Farm

On 21 June 1944 an aircraft on a local training flight crashed into farm buildings at Park Farm, killing five of the eight crew members.

The aircraft was a Short Stirling EH 940 from 1661 Heavy Conversion Unit, a training unit based at RAF Winthorpe near Newark, Nottinghamshire. Just minutes after takeoff the pilot reported a fierce fire in one of the port engines and asked for permission to return to land at the airfield but the request was denied because the circuit was very active with aircraft taking off or landing. The pilot tried to gain height, hoping he might be able to land at Wigsley.

At about 1800 feet above Fenton the pilot's luck ran out as the other port engine lost power and stopped. The aircraft went into an uncontrollable diving turn to starboard and it crashed into farm buildings at Park Farm.

Local landowner Ian Gourley from Hall Farm, Kettlethorpe, remembered the incident well. "I was working in a nearby field when I heard a strange noise which appeared to be getting louder and louder so I looked up and saw a large aircraft at rooftop height heading towards me, with flames and smoke pouring from one of its wings. My immediate thoughts were that the aircraft was going to hit a row of 40ft high poplar trees which were only a few feet from the house at Hall Farm, but luckily it missed them. The aircraft disappeared behind the house and the next thing I heard was a loud crash, then I saw some smoke and flames coming from some nearby farm buildings."

Tom Cox, who lives at Saxilby, also has vivid memories of the crash: "I was working in the yard at Park Farm on a tractor which would not start. I went into one of the sheds for a cup of tea and while pouring it out I heard a terrific crash and the shed I was in collapsed on top of me. Then there was an unbearable rush of heat and the next thing I remember was crawling out of the shed through an opening in the side.

"Once I was outside I was amazed to see the full extent of the tragedy. The fuselage of the Stirling had split open in the centre and I saw some of the crew escaping from the stricken bomber. We tried to help get the crew out of the front of the plane but the flames were so fierce we could not reach them and they perished in the flames. I will never forget the vivid memories of the crash at Park Farm as long as I live."

At the inquiry into the crash the Board was told that the pilot, Flying Officer Bradbury, was on his first flight with a full crew. The Stirling had flown a total of 256 hours up to the time of the crash and had carried out six sorties with 15 Squadron, four sorties with 218 Squadron and a further ten sorties with 1661

A Short Stirling Mk III EH 940 bomber, similar to the one that crashed

HCU up to the time of the crash. The RAF Board of Inquiry listened to all the evidence and ruled that the crash was caused by failure of a cylinder head stud and inoperative power plant fire extinguishers. Fg Off Bradbury was exonerated from any blame for the crash.

The crew of the ill-fated bomber aircraft:

- Fg Off Frederick Shaw Bradbury, RAF Volunteer Reserve, died aged 23
- Fg Off (Air Bomber) George Wallace Rankin, died aged 30
- Plt Off William Robert Clayton, died aged 30
- Sgt (Air Gunner) William Henry Miller, RAF Volunteer Reserve, died aged 27
- Sgt Joseph Albert Micallef, RAF Volunteer Reserve, died aged 19
- Sgt F Daubles, survived, injuries unknown
- Sgt T W Farrell, survived, injuries unknown
- Sgt A M McClune, survived, injuries unknown

Aerial view of the crash site at Park Farm, taken c1970, also showing the location of the recent wreckage

This was pilot Frederick Bradbury's first flight with a full crew. Before volunteering for service he was an employee in the Ways and Works Department of the Argentine Railways, living at Lomas de Zamora, near Buenos Aires.

Local residents formed the 'Trentside Memorial Group' to establish the memorial at Laughterton, the key feature of which is a propeller blade taken from the crashed aircraft. Standing l to r: David Westgarth, Phil Robinson, David Willey; seated l to r: Lynne Peters, Ian Gourley, & Sheila Eyton-Williams. Absent is well-known local aviation artist, Jack Larder.
(Photo taken c1994 by Keris Eyton-Williams, son of Sheila.)

The following is the text of a letter dated 28 June 1944, to Phyllis Moore (late mother of well-known local farmer Andrew Arden) who is commended for giving assistance at the scene of the crash.

Dear Miss Moore,

It has been brought to my notice that you helped to pull the NCO Rear Gunner out of the turret of the aircraft which unfortunately crashed from this Unit and burst into flames at Kettlethorpe on 21 June 1944.

I wish to thank you for the very prompt manner in which you acted and for the efficient way you managed to get hold of towels and water etc. from an adjacent farmhouse.

Your will to help has won my admiration and that of all ranks on this Unit.

You will I know, be distressed to hear that the Sergeant passed away shortly afterwards.

Yours sincerely,
J H Woodin
Group Captain, Commanding, RAF Station, WINTHORPE

David Willey, *Saxilby*

(With grateful thanks to Andrew Arden and Steve Jackson who provided supporting material for this article.)

Drinsey Nook at War

The little hamlet of Drinsey Nook is located several miles west of Saxilby, Lincoln at the junction of the A57 and the A156. The A57 runs from Liverpool to Lincoln and the A156 runs from this point to Gainsborough. The Fossdyke canal runs alongside the right-hand side of the junction.

At the beginning of World War Two and with the threat of invasion, in common with the rest of the country, all the road signs were taken down around Drinsey Nook, however to date the road signs around Drinsey Nook have never been replaced.

In the early hours of Saturday the 16th of May 1942 a Handley Page Hampden bomber crashed in the field across the Fossdyke canal opposite the hamlet of Drinsey Nook.

The Hampden, serial number P2120, was based at

the 16th Operational Training Unit at Upper Heyford, Oxfordshire and was on a night cross-country navigational training exercise when the pilot lost control in cloud and crashed from a height of 8,000 feet. The aircraft went into a violent flat spin, crashed and burst into flames on impact into the field, killing three of the four crew onboard.

Wartime Saxilby Police Constable Albert 'Tabb' Smith was first on the scene. Tabb Smith recalls: *"I was called out just after midnight to investigate the report of an aircraft crashing in flames, the location of the crash was very vague. However, eventually I located the crash in a field opposite Drinsey Nook corner on the Saxilby side of the river. The only access to the field was by cycling down to the end of West Bank, Saxilby and then walking crossing several fields.*

As I neared the end of West Bank I could see the aircraft well-ablaze in the field and as I approached the field

A Handley Page Hampden bomber, similar to the one that crashed at Drinsey Nook

gate I could see a shadowy figure lit by the flames of the burning aircraft, walking towards me carrying a large bundle. As he got closer I eventually saw it was an airman with a white parachute tucked under his left arm.

The airman seemed to be very dazed and he was nursing a very badly cut lip, he managed to tell me his name 'Sgt Mullaine' and that he had jumped to safety just minutes before the aircraft crashed. Sadly the rest of the crew of three had not been able to get out and they had all perished in the flames. I noticed that he spoke with a soft Canadian accent. I looked after him until help came."

The three crew killed were removed from the wreckage and buried with full military honours at St John the Baptist's Church, Scampton, three days later.

The Crew
▶ 116479 Flying Officer William Henry PARR
  RAF 25 Pilot
  Weston-super-Mare, England
▶ R/83189 Flight Sergeant David Charles MacNAB
  RCAF Observer
  Windsor, Ontario, Canada
▶ R/68423 Flight Sergeant Kenneth Gilbert McKEE

RCAF 21 WO/AG Ingersoll, Ontario, Canada
▶ Flight Sergeant MULLAINE RCAF WO/AG
  (no more details)

For many years afterwards on the anniversary of the crash, the father of the skipper of Hampden P2120, Fg Off Parr, made a pilgrimage from his home in Weston-super-Mare to visit the crash site and lay flowers on his son's grave at the Scampton war grave burial ground.

Even to this day when the conditions are right (a heavy dew) the area in the field where the aircraft crashed can be clearly seen as the soil is a slightly different colour to the rest of the field.

The headstone of Flying Officer William Henry Parr, one of the pilots killed in the crash. All three servicemen were buried at St John the Baptist's Church, Scampton

The Terrible Tale of Tom Otter

The Gibbeting of Tom Otter

Tom Otter's gibbet stood on the edge of Saxilby Moor in the 19th century, close by the B1190 Doddington Road, near Saxilby, known as Tom Otter's Lane.

Thomas Temporel, alias Tom Otter, was a navvy, employed on the Old Swanpool, near Lincoln. He was 28-years-old, had a wife and child living at Southwell, Notts and was hanged at Lincoln in 1806 for the murder of a young woman, Mary Kirkham of North Hykeham, to whom he had been bigamously married for just one day.

He had made Mary pregnant and the local authorities, unaware of his marital status, forced the marriage in order that the child should not become chargeable

to the parish. The ceremony took place on Sunday, 3 November 1805 in the presence of the parish constables.

After the wedding the pair made their way to Lincoln and the next morning Mary's body was found close to Doddington Road with a blood-stained hedge stake lying nearby.

An inquest was held at Saxilby on Tuesday 5 November and the next day Tom Otter was committed to Lincoln Castle on the charge of murder, confessed and was executed at Lincoln on 14 March 1806.

It was the custom that criminals condemned to be gibbeted should be measured for their irons before execution, but he was so violent that the blacksmith was unable to perform this task. His body was

↑ *Banns of Marriage for Tom Otter and Mary Kirkham*

brought from Lincoln and hung in irons on a gibbet 30 feet high, erected about 100 yards from the place where the body of Mary Kirkham was found, as an example to others.

The crowds came early to see the event and turned it into a festive occasion. Some years later when the jawbones had become sufficiently bare to leave a cavity between them, a willow-biter or blue titmouse built its nest in it. The discovery of nine fledglings gave rise to this poem:

There were nine tongues within one head,
The tenth went out to seek for bread,
To feed the living within the dead.

The gibbet, which was weakened by chipping off pieces of wood for tobacco stoppers and other mementoes, was blown down in the spring of 1850, having stood for 44 years. After lying for many years at Saxilby the remains of the post were made into

a chair and the head, leg irons and the hook used to gibbet Tom Otter are now on display at Doddington Hall.

Ghosts and Legends of Lincolnshire and the Fen Country, Polly Howat, Countryside Books, 1992

The gibbet, with what was left of Tom inside, stood in its lonely spot, with only the occasional gypsy camp for company, until 1850, when a gale brought it crashing down

Drinsey Nook Recent History

1936: Mr & Mrs Harold Whitworth are running a successful motor repair business and petrol sales. The petrol pumps are right on the side of the main A57 road, so any car filling up has to park on the main road as there is nowhere else to pull into.

1947: Mr Harold Whitworth died unexpectedly, then the garage is taken over by Mr & Mrs Harry Phipps who have come up from Littlehampton.

1955: The garage and petrol sales are taken over by Mr Miller who also has a garage at Scampton at the top end of Tillbridge Lane. Joe Richardson is put in charge at Drinsey Nook. The petrol sales are then

closed down and are moved to a new purpose-built petrol station at the end of Tom Otters Lane, which is still there today.

In the early 1960s the garage and buildings were purchased by Mr Paddy Fay, who then operated a land drainage business from the premises. Joe Richardson stays on as his engineer.

1992: Paddy Fay dies and the land drainage business closes. Since then there have been several businesses including pine furniture and inkjet recycling operating from there.

Prisoner of War Camp

 This building is believed to be the main cook house

This building is believed to be
Another view of what potentially is the main cook house

According to our information this was the wash house at the POW

Drinsey Nook had a prisoner of war camp. It was built at the end of 1942 and housed Italian prisoners of war.

Guarded by British soldiers security was quite lax as each morning they would go to various farms around the area to work. At the end of the war it was converted into a German resettlement camp for German people who chose to stay.

One such man was Hans Schipke who was in the German Navy on a U-boat and was initially held in Camp 52 in Retford before moving to Drinsey Nook at the end of the war. He soon fell in love with a lady called Joan Baker. They married and settled in Fenton where they lived until Hans passed away a few years ago. His wife Joan remembers her husband as a wonderful father and husband who is now sadly missed.

Hans Schipke (right) with his friend and fellow POW Ludwig in Fenton, 1946

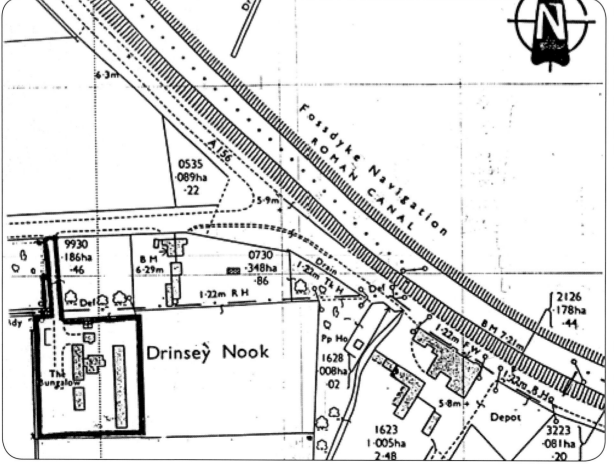

A map of Drinsey Nook with the POW camp circled

DRINSEY NOOK & PARK FARM
IN PICTURES

Not many pictures exist of Drinsey Nook, here are a selection showing the buildings that exist to this day along with a sailing barge.

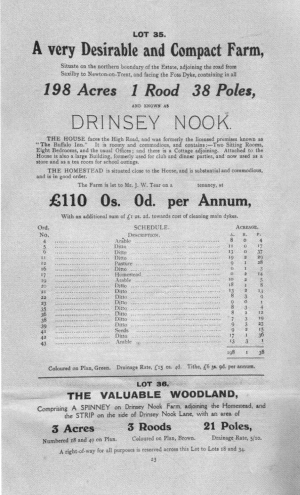

LOT 35.

A very Desirable and Compact Farm,

Situate on the northern boundary of the Estate, adjoining the road from
Saxilby to Newton-on-Trent, and facing the Foss Dyke, containing in all

198 Acres   1 Rood   38 Poles,

AND KNOWN AS

DRINSEY NOOK.

THE HOUSE faces the High Road, and was formerly the licensed premises known as
"The Buffalo Inn." It is roomy and commodious, and contains :—Two Sitting Rooms,
Eight Bedrooms, and the usual Offices ; and there is a Cottage adjoining. Attached to the
House is also a large Building, formerly used for club and dinner parties, and now used as a
store and as a tea room for school outings.

THE HOMESTEAD is situated close to the House, and is substantial and commodious,
and is in good order.

The Farm is let to Mr. J. W. Tear on a   tenancy, at

£110 0s. 0d. per Annum,

With an additional sum of £1 2s. 2d. towards cost of cleaning main dykes.

Ord. No.	Description.	A.	R.	P.
4	Arable	8	0	4
5	Ditto	11	0	17
6	Ditto	13	0	37
11	Ditto	19	2	29
15	Pasture	9	1	28
16	Ditto	0	1	3
17	Homestead	0	2	14
19	Arable	10	2	5
20	Ditto	18	1	8
21	Ditto	13	2	11
22	Ditto	8	3	0
23	Ditto	9	0	1
35	Ditto	8	3	4
36	Ditto	8	2	11
38	Ditto	7	3	19
39	Ditto	9	3	23
41	Seeds	9	2	15
42	Ditto	17	1	36
43	Arable	13	3	1
		198	1	38

Coloured on Plan, Green.   Drainage Rate, £15 0s. 4d.   Tithe, £6 3s. 9d. per annum.

LOT 36.
THE VALUABLE WOODLAND,

Comprising A SPINNEY on Drinsey Nook Farm, adjoining the Homestead, and
the STRIP on the side of Drinsey Nook Lane, with an area of

3 Acres   3 Roods   21 Poles,

Numbered 18 and 40 on Plan.   Coloured on Plan, Brown.   Drainage Rate, 5/10.

A right-of-way for all purposes is reserved across this Lot to Lots 18 and 34.

23

FENTON

Fenton is a small hamlet half a mile from Kettlethorpe, on the A156 Lincoln to Gainsborough road. The name Fenton is derived from the Old English fenn+tun, or 'farmstead in a fen or marsh'.

Early residents of Fenton

Fenton.

VILLAGE TALES

Down on the farm in the 1950s

An excerpt from rare film of farming in Fenton in the 1950s can be found on our community website, *www.trentsidelinks.org*. The shots of farming activity of the period, including threshing machines and horse-drawn seed drilling, were taken by the late Geoff Lidgett of Poplar Farm, Fenton, and are featured in the Bygone Lincoln DVD2 (second of a series of three).

Geoff grew up in a farming family in Fenton in the 1920s and '30s and bought Poplar Farm in 1948, the year of his marriage to Sarah. He saw the traditional practices of his industry give way to rapid mechanisation. From the late 1940s until the mid-50s he took a number of films, both 9.5mm and 16mm. They featured the farming practices of the day, old and new, and included many shots of the farm workers.

In 2002, Andrew Blow, of Blow by Blow Productions and former Yorkshire TV staffer, heard about Geoff's films and approached him for access to the material. Andrew and his associates transferred both film formats to video tape to enable Geoff and his family to see the material on VHS and DVD.

Andrew has the following recollections of Geoff:

"Geoff had a lifelong interest in tractors and could immediately name the make and model of any that appeared in the old footage. I was privileged to record his comments when I played the material back to him

Sarah Lidgett, wife of the late Geoff, atop of a horse & cart deftly driven by George Sewell June 1931

Workers at Fenton

Poplar Farm as seen from the air in the 1950s. The farm is an amalgamation of a number of smaller farms acquired by the Lidgett family including White House Farm

for the first time and I am so pleased I did, for his instant recollections were so fresh and amusing that it was far better than writing a retrospective script. Geoff's memories on the soundtrack have been appreciated by many people.

"Another story I love about him was that he used to go to the Lincolnshire Show to see the latest farm implements and adaptations — and then go back to the farm to try and modify his own equipment to reflect the latest gear, rather than spend thousands of pounds on new equipment. I heard about Geoff and his films in a most amazing way. I went into Burkitt's electrical and radio shop in Steep Hill to get something technical for my filming work. A man in the shop recognised me purely because of my voice, which he'd heard on Bygone Lincoln. This turned out to be Dave Willey of Saxilby, who was Geoff's postman. Dave asked Geoff if I could approach him and that's how the material became available today."

Andrew has edited a portion of the farming material for online use by Trentside Links following a suggestion by Sue Eyton-Williams of Fenton, daughter of the late Geoff. Sue and husband Keris continue to run Poplar Farm and maintain the family farming tradition.

Ellis Lidgett, Geoff's father, with horse & trap & family members

Fenton Practice Bombing Range

Towards the end of the Second World War the Royal Air Force set up a practice bombing range on land owned by the Gourley family of Kettlethorpe.

It was in 1943 that the Air Ministry commandeered 11.5 acres of land for the range, in the lowland area of the Trentside marshes running down to the River Trent between Fenton and Laughterton. The range target was a large concrete triangle with a lighting gantry mounted on top that illuminated the target during nighttime bombing practice.

RAF personnel controlled the range from two observation (Nissen) huts. The huts were located at the end of two farm tracks for easy access, accessible from the A1133 road between Torksey Lock and Laughterton.

One of the observation huts would be designated

the master and the other as slave. The master would have the primary sighting equipment and a generator to supply electricity for the target and hut lighting. A field telephone system linked it to the slave hut, which was some distance away on the edge of what is now the Millfield Golf complex.

The range was not manned all the time but when it was red flags would be hoisted to show that the range was live and in use. During a practise bombing run the aircraft would be allotted a time window to practise on the range and communication with the aircraft would be by either an Aldis signal lamp or Very signal pistol, the sort of things that often feature in old war films. The aircraft would fly over the target at a prearranged height and release an 8 or 11.5lb practice bomb towards the target. As the bomb landed it would emit a large plume of smoke and the two observation huts would take bearings to calculate the exact location and thus accuracy of the bomb drop.

The bombing range closed shortly after the war and the land was released back for agricultural use. The concrete or stone target was broken up and the resulting rubble used to provide bridges for crossing the dykes. The only remaining part of the range that is obvious today is the base of the master observation hut which now regularly supports a straw stack.

Colin Watson Recalls - Fenton Practice Bombing Range

We spoke to Colin Watson in connection with the Fenton practice bombing range because he had wartime memories. Colin is proprietor of the Millfield Golf Complex on part of which the range once stood. He moved from nearby Newton to the Nissen hut that served as the 'slave hut' of the practice bombing range. One amusing anecdote he recalled was that the prisoners of war had their meals brought to them each day. However, although there was an order to

deliver meals each day there clearly wasn't one for bringing back the used dinner plates and so they just piled up outside the hut. One day a horse came over and in helping itself to the leftovers crushed all the plates. Well, that's one way to deal with the washing up!

There was also the time when a Lancaster and the blast of the crash blew out the windows at the rear of the observation hut.

At nearby Headen there was a PoW camp where the German prisoners were employed in clearing hedges and dykes and such other farming and land maintenance work. They were good workers and following the war a number of them settled and married locally. One of the things they did was to build earthworks and dig trenches to deter enemy glider aircraft from landing.

Lancaster Aircraft Crash at Trentside Marshes

Whilst on my post-round on a sunny spring morning in 1993 I turned the corner on to the farm road leading to Poplar Farm, Fenton. Farmer Geoff Lidgett met me as he was coming out of the farm workshop and in his hand he had a large piece of twisted aluminum sheet that he had been removing from some farm machinery. He then told me that during the war a bomber had crashed and blown up in the Trentside marshes next to his land sending shards of metal all over the fields and occasionally, while working the fields, they still picked up bits in the farm machinery. I have always been interested in local history and WW2 aviation so this story really interested me, therefore I decided to find out what the bomber was, what had caused it to crash and what had happened to the crew. Over the following weeks I searched for information relating to the crash and eventually I found in a book a reference to a Short Stirling bomber from RAF Blyton that crashed and blew up in fields near the River Trent but the details were very sparse. Could this be the aircraft?

During the following weeks I spoke to as many local people as possible in Fenton and Laughterton about the crash. Lots of people remembered the loud explosion but not the details about the actual crash. Sarah Lidgett recalled that she had been at Poplar Farm that evening with her then boyfriend, Geoff Lidgett, and he had taken her home to Newton on Trent just before midnight. Sarah was then a member of the local firewatch and happened by chance to

look out of the attic window before going to bed. The attic window was a very good vantage point for looking for fires and Sarah recalls: "As I looked across the village I saw an aircraft completely engulfed in flames, falling from the sky. It disappeared behind the houses, then there was a blinding white flash followed by the sound of a massive explosion; it was awful."

Ian Gourley also knew about the crash and the location of the field but it was my discussion with Fred Dixon of Fenton that gave me the best lead. Fred remembered that the aircraft had crashed in the week following the August bank holiday weekend but he could not remember which year. Fred recalled, "It was harvest time and there were Lancaster parts in the corn". In the following week Ian Gourley kindly agreed to take me to the field where the aircraft crashed – he suggested the following Tuesday after work.

The day duly arrived and we set off for the crash site. On arrival we met up quite by coincidence with local farmer Andrew Arden, who happened to be farming land near to the crash site. Andrew said he was always finding small fragments of the aircraft while working the land. We did not have to look for long before we found some fragments, which looked like engine castings. I collected some parts and took them to Ian Hickling, Chief Engineer at Lincolnshire Aviation Centre, East Kirkby. Ian has spent a lifetime working on Rolls Royce Merlin engines, so without hesitation he confirmed that the parts were from a cylinder head on a Merlin 20 series engine. This confirmed that the crashed bomber was not the recorded Short Stirling, as that was fitted with Bristol Hercules radial engines; further reference numbers found on other fragments revealed conclusively that the aircraft was indeed an Avro Lancaster.

My friend Keith and I later searched for hours through documentation covering the total production of over 7000 Lancaster bomber airframe serial numbers. Avro Lancaster LM292 looked like a good match. Further evidence that this was the right aircraft came a few weeks later from the accident crash card held by the Air Historical Branch at RAF Hendon.

Avro Lancaster LM292 was built by Sir W G Armstrong Whitworth Aircraft Ltd at Whitley, Coventry. It was dispatched after flight tests to 103 Squadron based at the Lincolnshire airfield of Elsham Wold on 30 July 1944 and was coded PM-K-King. It replaced the previous PM-K-King ME799 aircraft which was lost on a mission to Stuttgart on 29 July 1944. The Lancaster LM292 was just seven days old when it crashed. Just after midnight on Tuesday 8 August 1944, in the week following the bank holiday weekend, people in the Trent Valley area were woken by a loud explosion as the Lancaster exploded on impact in a field adjacent to the Fenton inland RAF practice bombing range near the River Trent (see earlier in this issue). LM292 was one of seventeen Lancasters dispatched at 21.20 hours from RAF Elsham Wold to destroy a German stronghold at Fontenay-le-Mamion in France. The outbound flight went without incident but having reached the target area they were turned back by the master bomber, still with their 15,000lb bomb load, due to poor visibility caused by smoke haze and low cloud. A short while later, while crossing the French coast on its way back to base, the aircraft was hit by flak, which started a serious fire in the starboard outer engine.

The skipper of LM292 was Fg Off George Brown RCAF. He, ably assisted by flight engineer Sgt John Corless, tried desperately to extinguish the engine fire but they were unable to contain it and the engine started to misfire and lose power. Eventually Brown had to shut down the engine and feather the propeller.

The Lancaster at this time was at 18,000ft with a fire now raging in the starboard wing and with its full bomb load still on board. It started to lose height rapidly. At 14,000ft the aircraft went into a sudden spiral dive with Brown and Corless fighting to regain control and level the aircraft. They managed to eventually get the Lancaster straight and level at about 9,000ft for a short time, and, when about one mile west of Saxilby, Brown gave the order to abandon the aircraft.

Out bailed Robinson, Sandberg, Porter, Hurley and Vickery from the rear door. They parachuted into fields around Hardwick. On landing Fg Off Robinson ended up hanging by his parachute harness from the roof of a barn at Highfield Farm, Hardwick, with a bull in the pen below him. Moments later the stricken Lancaster plummeted earthwards into the Trentside Marsh and on impact with the ground blew up, killing George Brown and John Corless.

The large crater and the wreckage, strewn over several fields, caused many problems for the recovery teams in their search for bodies. It was days later when a farm worker found the body of Fg Off George Brown in a hedge some way from the point of impact. He was laid to rest in the war graves plot at the Stonefall Cemetery in Harrogate, Yorkshire.

The body of Sgt John Corless was never found. His name is honoured on panel 215 at the Runnymede Memorial in Englefield Green, Egham, Surrey.

My thanks to Lady Helen Nall, George Vickery, Winnie Corless and LAHC at East Kirkby, who in various ways helped to make this article possible.

The Stackyard Barn

This barn was used by the Gelder family of Newton on Trent for grinding corn. The left-hand side before the roof was put on was used to house a traction engine to spin the grinding wheels. Bags of wheat were shoved through the door you see on the second floor. Cows were milked below that floor. The offshoot second floor was a pigeon loft.

Photo taken by Fred Dixon.
Converted to a residential dwelling by
Geoff Lloyd of Fenton in the 1960s.

FENTON IN THE NEWS

TRAGIC COINCIDENCES AT FENTON

THREE DEATHS WITHIN A WEEK

PAINFUL EVIDENCE AT CORONER'S INQUEST

LINCOLNSHIRE ECHO
WEDNESDAY, MAY 5TH, 1909

Dr. W.H.B. Brook and a jury sat at the Carpenters' Arms, Fenton, last evening, for the purpose of investigating a painful case, relative to the death of a newly-born male child found in a box in the house recently occupied by a Mrs. Pycock, who died that day week, and where daughter Jessie Ann, was removed to the Lincoln Hospital on the night of her mother's funeral and died in that institution on Monday afternoon.

The Coroner briefly repeated the facts to the jury, and pointed out that the case was one which required their very careful attention. Briefly the facts were that the body of a child had been found in a house in the village, and the question was how the child came by its death. They had also to find whether the child had actually lived and had a separate existence. If it was stillborn, then the matter did not come under the law further for the purposes of registration, although anyone who concealed its birth might be proceeded against.

The jury, of which Mr. W. Stevenson was the foreman, then viewed the body, after which P.C. (illegible), stationed at Fenton, stated that the previous day he went to the house of the late Harriet Pycock, in company with Joseph Crust, her son-in-law. On searching upstairs in the back bedroom he found, in a tin trunk containing several dress skirts and rags, the body the jury had viewed. It was wrapped in a window curtain, which was twisted round its neck. There was no one else in the house at the time, but there had been a sister of Jessie Pycock living with her and her mother. Mrs. Pycock died on Tuesday of last week, and was buried on Thursday. The older daughter was named Harriett and the younger one Jessie. The daughter Jessie had been taken ill and had to be taken to the Lincoln Hospital on Thursday night, and died there on Monday.

Supt. F - *Was the curtain tied more than once round the neck? - Yes, three times.*
Was it tight? - Yes, very tight.
Do you think if the child had been alive, it would have been sufficiently tight to stop breathing? - Oh yes.

Joseph Crust, farm manager, of Fenton, described to the police coming to his house on the matter, and to going with the constable, who found the body in his (witness a) presence.

The Coroner: *Have you any reason to believe whose child this was? - I have only the reason to believe it was the one's who had been going out with Jessie.*

Witness added that his sister-in-law Jessie was taken ill last Thursday, but he could not say he had noticed anything, except that for a day or two he had had suspicions, but no more. Both his sisters-in-law had been about as usual on Tuesday and Wednesday, and had assisted in nursing their mother.

The Coroner: *Was your sister Jessie engaged to be married? - No sir : not that I am aware of.*
Did your sister-in-law attend Mrs. Pycock's funeral? - No sir : Jessie did not, that was the day she was taken ill.

Dr. P.H. Rainbird, of Saxilby, stated that he had been and examined the body, which weighed 9lbs. He should say it had been dead for two or three days. He could not tell that it had had a separate existence from its mother. It did not show any signs of having died of haemorrhage. The cloth was wrapped tightly twice round the neck, and then twisted - not tied. On the Thursday night and following the death of Mrs. Pycock, he received a note calling him to see Jessie Pycock. He arrived about nine o'clock, and found her condition so serious from blood poisoning that he ordered her immediate removal to Lincoln Hospital. He could not say positively that she had given birth to a child, but his suspicions were very strongly aroused.

Sergeant: *Was there any reason, doctor, if the child had had proper attention, that it should have died? - I must say, if it had had proper attention, it should have lived.*

It was rather a fine child, was it not? - Yes.

If it had been alive, do you think the cord round its neck would have caused death? - Yes.

It was sufficiently tight? - Sufficiently tight to stop breathing.

Dr. Liddell, Senior House Surgeon at the Lincoln County Hospital, stated that he did not think there was much chance of Jessie Pycock recovering when she was admitted. She died on the Monday afternoon from blood poisoning. She had given birth to a child within the past four days. The fact that her mother had died from erysipelas would very likely have something to do with her death from blood poisoning.

The Coroner summed up the case, and described it as a painful one. It was always painful to have to bring up anything which would cast reflection upon those who had passed away, but it was his duty to get to the bottom of the matter. Otherwise blame might have been put on those who were still living, and in fairness to those still alive, one had to go carefully into the whole matter. He thought the evidence was perfectly plain.

Without any lengthy deliberation, the jury came to the conclusion that the child was found dead, but that there was no evidence to show that it had had a separate existence.

LINCOLNSHIRE CHRONICLE

— OCTOBER 8 1875 —

Mary Gaunt landlady of the Carpenters' Arms, Fenton was charged with being drunk in her own house on the 22nd July. Evidence was given in support of the charge by PC Dennis, Wm. Worthington and Wm.Troop. Mr. Page for the defendant contended that the defendant was not drunk, but suffering from excitement and called Elizabeth A. Taylor, servant in the employ of defendant, in support of his statement. The bench however considered the case proved, and fined the defendant 10s...and £1. 4s.6d costs.

LINCOLNSHIRE ECHO SEPTEMBER 8, 1938

Fenton
Every Friday
Dance at the
Road House
(Carpenter's Arms. Fully licensed)
8.30 to 12.30
Bus leaves Broadgate 8.10pm
Tickets include Bus 2/-
Dance 1/-
Obtainable from Messrs. Jack Brentnall's music shop (next to Grand Cinema) and on bus
Special engagement of
TERENCE LITTLEWOOD'S DANCE ORCHESTRA

LAMB STOLEN IN FENTON

LINCOLNSHIRE ECHO SATURDAY JUNE 14 1913

A carter named Walter Parson aged 30 of Sheffield pleaded guilty to stealing a lamb belonging to John Gourley at Fenton, on May 4th. The evidence for the Crown showed that the accused visited Torksey on a Sunday excursion. He went to a field in Fenton & took away the lamb. In the evening the prosecutor, having missed the lamb, went to Torksey railway station where he saw prisoner who had the lamb under his coat. When he taxed him with the theft, the prisoner said he had picked it up. There was nothing against the accused previously and he was sent down for a month with hard labour.

MY STORY

Clare Anyan

My family's story in the Trentside area begins in Fenton in the 1880s. My great-grandmother moved there with her husband. They ran The Forge in Fenton (now a dwelling) and my great-grandfather, Richard Johnson Moore, was the blacksmith and they lived there with their family, three boys and two girls. When the youngest, my Aunt Ethel, was five months old my great-grandfather went to Lincoln market and never returned and nothing was heard of him from that point. As you can imagine in those times it was extremely tough for my great-grandmother but she persevered and hired a blacksmith to run the forge. Charles Lambert became the blacksmith and seven years later my great-grandfather was presumed dead and this is where my story takes a happier turn. My great-grandmother married Mr Lambert and continued to live happily at Yew Tree Cottage.

Clare's father Clarry at Lodge Farm Kettlethorpe 1958

My family had many happy memories in the Trentside area. My father Clarry was part of the Kettlethorpe scouts group and they met in the scout hut down Westmoor Lane, my father often recounted memories of the scout camps away to Mablethorpe!

Clare's father Clarry Moore, far left, with the Scouts from Fenton on a trip to Mablethorpe in 1928

Fenton Shop

My great-grandmother died in the 1930s but my family carried on living in Fenton and my grandfather, Charles Lambert, lived there with Aunt Ethel, Annie and Jack Formery (a lodger). My grandfather was a cycle agent and also stoned the roads and the family continued to live in Fenton until Aunt Ethel died in the 1960s. I recall the garden at Yew Tree Cottage being very beautiful with a lot of privet edgings, all very Victorian!

Relatives of Clare Anyan outside Yew Tree Cottage on Maltkiln Road.

My grandfather took the tenancy of nearby Lodge Farm in Kettlethorpe. My father originally wanted to take it over but could not secure the tenancy himself. We had many happy memories farming the land

and living in the local area and my father recalled once that during the war he also remembered the Dambusters flying over Kettlethorpe on their way to the Ladybower reservoir and he wondered what they were up to at the time.

My family enjoyed life in Kettlethorpe, often taking part and attending the many gardens fetes at Kettlethorpe Hall where we would play some of the games still played at today's modern fetes. My family continued to farm at Kettlethorpe for many years until they moved away to retire to Saxilby but the happy memories live on and I am delighted that I have been able to share these with you.

Fred Dixon

Always known as Fred, he was born on 3 March 1924 at Stallingborough near Grimsby, the son of Frederick Carter Dixon, a farm worker. His father rented a 60 acre farm at Nettleton, near Caistor, when Fred was a year old and moved to another 84 acre farm after six years. Many of the locals worked in the nearby ironstone mine and were yellow from the dust. Fred left school at 14 as he was needed to work on the farm. At the age of 16 they moved to Fillingham where his father took another farm (Chapel Farm) but they only stayed there a couple of years as his father would not sign a long lease. Fred was not called up, as most young men were, as farming was a reserved occupation along with coal mining. However, he played his part by joining the Home Guard and carrying out firewatch duties.

Fred's family home in Lincoln Rd, Fenton

Fred (front left), his father (back left), Sammy Anderson (front right) and the Land Army girls on a break at the farm

So it was in 1942 that the family moved to Fenton, father working for Ellis Lidgett, grandfather of Sue Eyton-Williams, and Fred working for Ernie Robinson, both farms being in Fenton. His father bought a house in Fenton that is now part of the house that Fred lived in. Ernie had land in various places locally, including the Laughterton marshes where there was a bombing range during the war. When bombing practise was in progress they had to leave their work and return later. One time a sheep had

an ear removed by a falling practice bomb, a really close shave! He remembered the aircraft crash in the marshes that is commemorated on the memorial in Laughterton, as he had to help remove debris and remains from among the corn. Fred worked for Mr Robinson for four years. Long after the war he remembers the occasion when there were nine ricks on fire in Robinson's stackyard.

During the war Fred rang the bells at Kettlethorpe church along with Len East who rang the middle bell and Harry Watson who rang the large bell. All three bells were rung until five minutes before the service and then just the large one tolled until the start of the service. They were rung for services, weddings, funerals and of course to celebrate the end of the war. He remembers they had to dig out

Fred at work on the Lidgett Farm with tractor & plough

heaps of sticks carried in by rooks that stopped the bells ringing (the wire netting was defective) and that a blue tit had a nest in the back of the clock. A Mr Scarborough played the organ, which had to be hand pumped in those days. Judge Langman resided at the hall, and Joan Baker (now Schipke) and Betty Good were maids.

Fred met Phylis May Sensicall at the chapel in Fenton (where her parents worshipped and paid pew money!) and they were married by Rev Holmes in 1947. The reception was in the village hall and they set up home at Rose Cottage opposite the Friendship Inn in Laughterton. He also changed employer, moving to the Lidgett farm as a tractor driver. After two years he moved back into the newly extended house in Fenton. In the atrocious weather of 1947 he was clearing snow for the council on Burton top road and could picture Maltkiln Road being flooded at the Brickyard Cottages end. Fred also remembered Harry Heath who worked at the pumping station at Torksey, working day and night to keep the water levels right. It was in 1947 following a hard winter with lots of water on the ground, when one day the banks burst at Spalford and the water levels rose and came up from the drains at Laughterton. Geoff Lidgett and his men, together with seven German prisoners of war, all went to Spalford to block the hole in the bank with sandbags and fill the bags of sand too. They all set off in Geoff's Bedford lorry but when they arrived at Spalford the front of the lorry fell into the drain and filled with water, luckily an RAF lorry towed it out. Geoff then had the job of walking all the way back to Fenton to get oil for his van. In 1949 he and Phylis had Kenneth John, who was born mentally handicapped. He spent time in St John's and Harmston but now resides in Middlefield House in Gainsborough, where Fred used to visit him.

After 10 years both Fred and his father moved work to Gainsborough, into engineering, for another 10 years before Fred moved to Bradshaw's of Sturton by Stow as a lorry driver until he retired at the age of 63. Never one to be idle he became a radio ham and used to contact Mir, the space station, regularly. His wife unfortunately died in 1998 and his sister, who lived in the same building, died in 2002. Always a keen gardener, Fred once had his picture in the Echo for growing a tomato that weighed a pound and three quarters — that's 791 grams in new money! He was a keen naturalist and bird watcher and used to go out most days despite having broken his hip and having limited mobility. Fred had never flown in a big plane but has flown in a microlite, a helicopter and twice in a glider.

So what has changed in Fenton while Fred has lived here? The butcher (Len Addison) is gone, along

Fred & his impressive tomato, as featured in the Lincolnshire Echo

with the post office within it. So is the blacksmith (Mr Lambert situated in the old forge on Maltkiln Road), the chapel, the carpenter shop (in Scotch Row on the site of the flats run by Mr Albert Jones) and Wilkinson's shop. There were also visits by Gelder's van, Jubb's van and the Curtis van. The bakery was closed when Fred arrived in Fenton, as was the saddlers and the cycle shop (11 Lincoln Rd). The Poor Hill Cottages were knocked down and replaced by what is now known as Chestnut House. The water for the cottages came from a communal pump next to where the memorial stands and it was referred to as the town pump. The house next to the chapel was once the police house and a Mr Jincks was the first policeman to be remembered living there, after he retired he was replaced by Mr Wilkinson. The same house was also a grocer's shop run by Ross Addison.

Back in those days the bus shelter at what was always known as Four Lane Ends was wooden and had been built by the scouts, evidently before health and safety regulations came into effect.

Fred sadly passed away on the 12th of August 2012 but we were delighted to be able to preserve his memories of his time in the area.

Loraine Rontree

On the 21st November 1958 I had just turned 11 when my parents, Ron and Maisie Hill, moved the family from Lea near Gainsborough to take over as landlord and landlady of the Carpenters Arms, my sister Barbara and brother Richard were six and four.

At that time I was still attending Lea Church of England school and remember going on the bus which I caught on the corner passing Scotch Row cottages where the flats now stand, and waiting outside the big house where Mr & Mrs Robinson lived. I later attended Sturton by Stow Secondary School and continued travelling on the bus. I soon began to feel more at home and started to make friends with other children travelling on the bus from Kettlethorpe, Laughterton and Newton.

There was no street lighting in the village then, but it seemed quite safe and I often used to walk in the dark down to Kettlethorpe to see my friend the late Linda Toyne, when we often attended functions in Kettlethorpe village hall; whist drives, beetle drives and dances. We also had Christmas parties and drama groups there. I was a member of Kettlethorpe Church Choir and I recall walking on a Sunday evening to church with Margaret and Dorothy Wilkinson for the evening service.

Linda and I, along with others, used to cycle to Newton to meet friends and go to the youth club at the vicarage which was run by the then vicar Mr Frank Woodford. We also used to go to Edgar's fish and chip shop, which if I recall was open on Tuesday and Friday evenings. On our way back home I remember some of the local lads we'd been with would secretly leave before us and jump out of the bushes on the straight road between Newton and Laughterton and scare us to death.

I remember school summer holidays and sneaking into Preston Farmers who had a large storage warehouse up Maltkiln Road. It stored sacks and sacks of animal feed all placed in different height piles. A few of us would creep in so that the warehouseman couldn't see us from his office which was up some steps on a raised platform. We'd spend as much time as we could get away with jumping from pile to pile, playing hide and seek, until we were found out and then we had to make a quick exit with our tails between our legs, but I remember what great fun it was and when a few days had passed we'd chance our luck again.

Those years went by so quickly but they were happy days.

Margaret Adcock

My earliest memory of living in the Trentside area was living with my two siblings (we were all born in the same house in Fenton). My younger brother, Frank Wilkinson was born in 1934, my elder sister, Dorothy Wilkinson was born in 1930 and I was born in 1931.

Fenton at the time was a very different place. My father ran the general shop and newsagents, there was a butcher (Addison's), a police house, a blacksmith, a joiner (Mr Jones, who also made coffins), a cobbler, a post office (run by Rosamund Addison) and of course the Carpenters Arms.

We all went to the Laughterton & Kettlethorpe C of E School which was situated in Laughterton (and is now a residential dwelling). I recall that milk was served to us in bottles and school life was a lot different. It was a primary school that you went to as an infant at age five and stayed there until you were 15, we often had to walk from Fenton to Laughterton to get to school and in all weathers too, we were often snowballed by the locals and we made our way through the snow and ice. If we were lucky we sometimes managed to catch the bus! In those days the heating in the school was powered by coke and then once the coke had been used up the ashes would be spread on the playground, I still have the marks on my knees from falling on it to this day!

The head teacher at the time was Mrs Pearce who lived at Newton on Trent and the helper was Miss Perry who lived in a bungalow on Newton Road in Laughterton, Miss Perry's sister was also head at Newton on Trent school at the time. There were probably 25 pupils who attended the school at the time from Fenton, Laughterton and Kettlethorpe.

During World War II my father was chairman of the parish meeting (at that time there was not a full parish council) from 1936 to 1969 and he was the billeting officer for when the evacuees came. I recall a busload coming from Armley in Leeds and my father had the difficult job of finding places for them. I remember the Lidgetts (farmers in Fenton) took two sisters in, Dorothy and Margaret McHale, and they had a daughter Heather, Mrs Lidgett was very kind to them and dressed them all in the same outfits! It was a very difficult time for the evacuees in all the upheaval and it took some time for them to settle in away from home. My mother would often look after the evacuees until a home could be found and would often feed and look after them until they were settled.

At the same time my father was also running the local shop in Fenton but because of the special work he was involved in during the war, and that he was a special constable, my mother could not run the shop on her own and so we had to close it down. One of my father's responsibilities was to visit the railway bridge at Torksey to check that no explosives had been planted there!

Fenton has changed a lot over the years. There used to be a row of houses opposite Addison's butchers called Scotch Row which was subsequently demolished and is where the flats now sit. We also had a parish pump in Fenton which was on Chestnut Corner (which is now where the war memorial sits), most people used the parish pump but we did have our own as well. I remember my father eventually filling the well up, concerned that we may fall down it at some point!

In 1938 we were one of the first houses to get electricity in Fenton, not everyone was able to install it at the time and still had to rely on candlelight and coal!

When I left school at Laughterton I later went to tech-college after the war. After leaving college and working at Beal's garage (now Arnold's 4x4 garage) on the A57 for four years where I served on the pumps and worked in the office, I went on from there to Wojna's egg farm in Fenton which was located just behind the Carpenters Arms. There was also a farmyard at that time and more chicken houses were built to keep up with demand.

I met my husband, Keith, when he used to come on holiday to Addison's in Fenton, we had known each other from a number of years and he was from Peterborough. His cousin used to live at Chestnut House and I used to drive her to church, one day she invited me for Sunday lunch at her house and unbeknown to me it was a bit of a blind date! We married in 1987 and I then worked for Lincolnshire County Council in the planning department until I retired.

Barbara Butler
(née Hill)

Memories of the Carpenters Arms
It was November 21st 1958 when the Hill family moved into the Carpenters Arms, Fenton. There was Ron and Maisie and their three children, Loraine, Barbara and Richard (affectionately known as Dick) 11, 6, and 4 years of age respectively. They had left a nice modern house in Lea, Gainsborough and arrived on a cold winter's day at a run-down pub which didn't even have a proper toilet. The facilities at that time were not only outside and round the back of the dancehall, but they consisted of a hole in the ground under a toilet seat, an earth toilet, outdated even for 1958! Barbara remembers that on that day there was even a vagrant pig rummaging in the kitchen!

Maisie was not one to be phased by this and she soon got the place spic and span and open to the public. At that time within the pub there was a little shop selling such basic items like tea, coffee and sweets. This was located where the ladies' toilets are now but when the pub was modernised in the 1960s the shop had to go, consequently the 'Ladies' took the place of the shop and so it was no more.

Maisie and Ron worked very hard and it wasn't long before they successfully put the Carpenters Arms and indeed, Fenton, on the map. Maisie was very enthusiastic and full of ideas. She was a born organiser and every spring she would have a trio or a jazz band to entertain the locals at the much talked-of dinner dance. People would come from far and wide, and despite few people in those days owning cars, they would be parked up and down the surrounding streets, such was the popularity of the dances. There generally wasn't much in the way of trouble but anyone misbehaving would have the formidable Maisie to answer to, she didn't take any messing about and was known to send potential troublemakers away with a flea in the ear. Sometimes, Mel, the local bobby, would arrive from Saxilby on his moped to check everything out. On a Friday night he used to come for his pie and pea supper on his way home, last port of call at the end of his shift.

Each year the Gainsborough Motor Company would attend on bonfire night for the Annual Tramp Supper, they would supply the fireworks and Barbara and Dick made the bonfire. They would bring tyres to put around the perimeter of the fire to keep it safely in place and the whole village would turn out for a wonderful communal gathering complete with live entertainment. In those days of course Bonfire Night was always celebrated on the 5th November so the party was often mid-week.

It soon became a very celebrated venue for weddings thanks to Maisie and her famous parties. She expertly provided the catering and was always booked up in advance, so much so that when Barbara got married there was only one date free in September 1972 and that was the 2nd, so that's the date it had to be. One of the villagers at the time remarked that Barbara's wedding was the best he'd ever been to! Maisie also organised Loraine's wedding in July 1967, she didn't stop at the Carpenters either, she arranged and catered for weddings elsewhere! The Rev Frank Woodford, vicar of Newton, was a regular patron and when his daughter Elizabeth got married Maisie organised the party at the vicarage in Newton-on-Trent. Barbara remembers going along to the vicarage on the day to help out. Perhaps Maisie set the trend for the modern day career of wedding planner! Ask anyone in the area about Maisie and everyone knew her, she had a wide circle of friends and even today people still remark to Barbara about the wonderful times that they had in the company of Maisie and Ron.

Maisie was renowned for her Christmas dinners that she cooked throughout December. There were no professional kitchen ranges like you would expect, just a small kitchen, one oven and one determined and talented lady! She would produce three course dinners which attracted local businesses for their annual get-together, many travelling from Lincoln. School teachers from Sturton School had their Christmas lunch in what was then the lounge bar (in those days the pub was divided into two small rooms),

a good time was had by all and they always came back again the following year.

Every Saturday night there was a dance with people coming from as far afield as Lincoln for the music, the Carpenters being one of only three venues in the Lincoln area in the 1960s. Of course there was no drink-driving ban in those days so friends would pile into cars and make their way to Fenton for their weekend entertainment and dancing. There were always live bands and two of the most popular went on to become quite famous in the 1960s. The Casuals had a number 1 hit with Jesamine, one of the most memorable iconic sounds of the 60s. One of the dads used to bring the lads from Lincoln to rehearse and Maisie always let them use the dancehall. Then there was Jimmy Crawford who used to come from Sheffield to play at the dances. He used to visit Little London at the weekends with his wife and her family, her brother was Howard Wilkinson who was once manager of Leeds United, they would spend their Saturday evenings at the Carpenters with Jimmy performing. He went on to form The Jimmy Crawford Blend and had two hits, one of them being I Love How You Love Me. Jimmy always drew large crowds, Maisie loved his music and used to go to his gigs in the area whenever she could.

Maisie and Ron were often awoken in the early hours of the morning by stones being thrown at the window by villagers-in-need. They were always willing to help people and being one of the very few car owners in the village they used to ferry people about whenever they could. Occasionally it would be someone's wife in labour and Ron would take them to the 'Maternity Home' in Willingham-by-Stow. Sometimes it would be a routine hospital appointment in Lincoln and Barbara and Dick would go along for a ride, such was the novelty having parents with a car in those days!

Maisie and Ron ran the Carpenters Arms for 14 years and loved every minute of it, they threw their heart and soul into it and made it the place to be. They moved on in November 1972 when they moved to Lincoln, leaving for a quieter life. They had a fantastic time at the Carpenters but it had been hard work and they were ready for a change. Tragically Dick was killed in a road accident in September 1976 on the same day that Barbara's youngest son was born. Ronnie died in November 1985 closely followed by Maisie in March 1986, just as she was to celebrate her 60th birthday party with family and friends. Sadly, all three lie next to each other in the graveyard at Kettlethorpe Church.

FENTON IN PICTURES

Residents of Fenton stood outside the Carpenters Arms seen on the right

The old terraced houses as seen from the entrance to Maltkiln Road which have now been replaced by the flats

An aerial view of Fenton taken before the Addison Place development and before further development on Lincoln Road, the large maltkilns can still be seen to the left of the picture

Family members outside the Addison house on Maltkiln Road

In this picture Addison's butchers shop can be seen on the left looking down Maltkiln Road

Residents of Fenton at the turn of the last century

42

The old maltkilns, Fenton, prior to demolition

The old maltkilns, Fenton, towards the end of the demolition

An aerial view of Fenton. You can still see the Maltkilns in this picture and this was taken prior to some of the housing developments from the 1980s onwards.

A picture taken from number 9 Lincoln Road showing the white cottages which have since been demolished

An old property in Fenton which was demolished to make way for Melway & Barley House on Maltkiln Road

An early picture of Fenton looking from the end of Lincoln Road towards Lincoln with the terraced houses on the right which now now been replaced with the flats

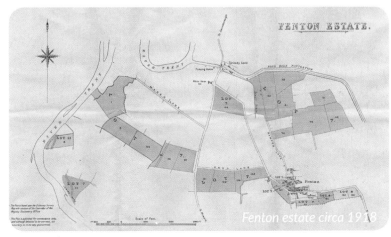
Fenton estate circa 1918

A view from the old terraced house towards Lincoln with Addison's house on the left

Land Army girls working on the farm in Fenton

The old Wesleyan chapel on Lincoln Road, now used as business premises

The derelict house that was once 4 Maltkiln Road and was situated in between Fenton House and Yew Tree Cottage and was demolished some years ago

In February 1795 the Trent bank at Spalford was breached and nearly 8.000 hectares of land to the west of Lincoln was flooded, this map shows with the shaded area how the Trentside region was hit and how some areas managed to avoid the floods.

Hay baling in Fenton

 Addison's butchers shop in operation on Maltkiln Road

Working on Poplar Farm farm in the 1950s

 The late Geoff Lidgett of Poplar Farm had had own pet crow, it was so tame it would sit on his shoulder and wouldn't leave Geoff's side!

The 1811 barn in Fenton, now converted to a private dwelling

Sue Eyton-Williams of Poplar Farm having a riding lesson

Children of the Gate Burton area
(full image & caption page 53)

GATE BURTON

Gate Burton is a small village that lies between Marton and Knaith. As you drive northwards from Marton on the A156 to Gainsborough you can't help but notice the splendid Gate Burton Hall, crowning a field that rises to the right.

A little further up the A156 and to the left is the Chateau sat charmingly atop a mound. But for these two features you might easily pass through the village without noticing it, but despite its small size Gate Burton has a rich history.

VILLAGE TALES

The Old Schoolhouse

The old schoolhouse in Clay Lane, Gate Burton, was originally provided and supported by William Hutton in 1851. It is mentioned in Kelly's Directory 1876 and in the 1889 edition it reports there were 30 pupils with an average attendance of 22. By 1905 it had become a council school with 55 pupils and had an average attendance of 30. The old schoolhouse has since been converted and is now a private domestic residence.

We spoke to Mr Graham Worrell who was a pupil at the school in the 1940s/50s and he shared some of his memories with us. He has fond memories of Mrs Torr, his teacher, whom you can see in the photograph (*overleaf*), taken around 1952/3. Mrs Torr was very motherly, said Graham, and he recalls a time when he was in hospital for a long period and Mrs Torr visited him. On one of her visits Graham had asked if the flag at school had been flown lately and Mrs Torr promised to fly it in honour of his return to school and sure enough she kept her word. He seemed to recall that apart from her normal teaching duties she sometimes cooked the school dinners too! Mrs

Graham Worrell (centre) and his brother on the farm at Gate Burton

Glassbrook from Wigan was Mrs Torr's successor and Graham recalled she was rather sterner.

The school entered lots of music festivals and won trophies for their efforts. The school was finally closed in the early 1960s when a new school was built at Marton.

Mrs Torr (centre) surrounded by staff and schoolchildren at her retirement party, sat in the armchair that was her retirement gift.

Old Pupil Makes His Home in Village School

The following news item appeared in 'The News', 12 July 1968:

'A Gate Burton farmer who attended the village school as a child now lives with his wife in the old school building, now converted into an attractive home.

The couple are Mr & Mrs Graham Worrell, Mr Worrell being a farmer with his father & brother on the estate of Mr & Mrs J.E. Sandars of Gate Burton Hall.

Mr Worrell and his wife, Gillian, were looking for a house before they were married last September and were offered the tenancy of the old school building, near the Hall entrance drive, by Mr & Mrs Sandars. Use of the building as a Church of England School ended nearly two years ago and rather than see it fall into disrepair, Mr & Mrs Sandars decided to have it converted into a dwelling-house.

Conversion took about eight months to complete and said Mrs Worrell: "It was ready for us to move into immediately after we got married. We are both delighted with the house; it has been made extremely comfortable."

Apart from new rectangular frames to replace the church-like arched windows there has been very little alteration to the exterior of the old school, though a great deal of work has been done to the interior.

New walls have been built in the former large and lengthy classroom to provide a spacious lounge, bedroom and bathroom. Ceilings to a standard height have been fitted, obscuring the high roof timbers and creating another storey.

The upper part is not used, however, the conversion transforming the building into a bungalow-type dwelling. The old school entrance has been converted to form an attractively decorated hall from which a passage through to a rear door separates the lounge and other rooms from a modern streamlined kitchen and larger bedroom.

Mr & Mrs Worrell have done much to make their home bright and attractive, with fitted carpets in the lounge, bedrooms and elsewhere, and furniture and furnishings in accordance with a predetermined scheme. A feature of the lounge is the fireplace which Mr & Mrs Worrell themselves chose.

Work on the conversion was carried out by Mr Sandars' estate maintenance staff. Said Mr Worrell: "This house is very nice and comfortable. We are very happy here, it is a fine conversion."

The old school in Clay Lane Gate Burton, now a private home

Gate Burton Hall

Gainsborough lawyer Thomas Hutton bought the Gate Burton estate from the 3rd Earl of Abingdon (a Bertie and descendant of the Earls of Lindsey) in 1744. It is built of yellow handmade bricks and is in the Well Wapentake area of Lincolnshire - a land division mentioned in the Domesday Book. It continued to be owned by the Hutton family until 1908 when the house and part of the estate were sold to John ('Jack') Drysdale Sandars and his wife Maud who bought back much of the land that used to belong to the estate.

Maud was daughter of the 5th Lord Graves who was a successful portrait painter and is now buried at

Gate Burton. Incidentally, the first Lord Graves was a vice admiral in the navy who was a great supporter of, and older than, Lord Horatio Nelson who got him an Irish barony.

Jack and Maud had two children - Eric (born 1906) and Rosemary (born 1910). The latter had a son, John Burke, who also married a Rosemary and the couple are the present owners of Knaith Hall in Knaith.

In 1913/14 the hall was substantially altered and enlarged, including a new entrance and a row of rooms on the north side, together with a large new eastern section, plus the addition of the imposing north front, built in neo-Georgian style by a British architect with

Mr & Mrs Sandars regularly organised music festivals. Could this be a picture from such an event?

the colourful name of Detmar Jellings Blow. Blow was a friend of Edwin Lutyens and had been mentored by John Ruskin. He designed many large country houses and other famous buildings including Bramham Park, Government House in Salisbury, South Africa, the east end of King's College Chapel Cambridge, and Selfridges department store in London. Blow's clients were largely high-ranking members of the British aristocracy. Later in his career he became estates manager to the Duke of Westminster, an appointment which had an ignominious ending for Blow, when we has dismissed following allegations of defrauding the duke's Grosvenor estate in London.

If the rebuilding of the south front of Gate Burton Hall was also intended it did not come about, as the *Great War* intervened. However, further alterations were made by Mr Sandars' son, the late Colonel J E (Eric) Sandars, in 1934, at the same time removing some ugly Victorian additions to the south front. The Sandarses (Eric and wife Margaret) occupied the house for some 42 years until Eric's death in 1974 (their notable contribution was the landscaping of the

The late Mrs Margaret Sandars with daughter Clare and Clare's daughter and grandchild

gardens) following which the house and estate were sold. Many of the houses neighbouring the hall were owned by the estate and a row of estate workers' cottages may be seen on the right just before you enter the south gate of the estate.

In his book *Lincolnshire Houses* (1999) Henry Thorold recalls an occasion when he was lunching with Colonel and Mrs Sandars in 1963. Reflecting on the occasion in 1993, he continues *"On the far bank of the Trent the enormous power station of West Burton was rising - a threat to the view. On this side of the river the gardeners were feverishly planting trees, a copse or two, and so on, to conceal this monster. Now, thirty years later...the planting has worked. The power station is invisible from the house".*

The Hall as a Maternity Unit
It is known locally that during the Second World War the hall was used as a place for mothers to have their babies. The following is an extract from a newspaper of the time:

'3,175 babies born at war-time emergency home'
At the outbreak of the war, the Ministry of Health decided to open emergency maternity homes for the reception of expectant mother from vulnerable areas. Colonel Sandars, owner of Gate Burton Hall, very generously offered use of the hall for this purpose and the Ministry asked Lindsey County Council to furnish and equip the hall as a maternity home and manage it on their behalf. A management committee with Councillor C F Everat as chairman was appointed and the home was fully equipped with 40 maternity beds and the necessary theatres, isolation wards etc.

The County Council were instructed by a telegram received from the Ministry on 31 August 1939 to open the home and since that date 3,175 babies have been born there. Although by far the greatest numbers of mothers come from Hull, a number of women from other parts of the country were also received. Thanks to the excellent work of the medical staff, Miss Greenley the matron and all the members of the staff, the maternal mortality rate in the home was lower than at any similar home in the country. Miss Greenley was one of the superintendent midwives in Hull and an ideal woman for the job, quiet-voiced, neat in her person and with twinkling eyes that gives testimony to that sense of humour which is part and parcel of her very human makeup.

In addition there are 14 pupil midwives in training, because the training school for midwives from Hedon Road is also evacuated here. For them the hospital is part one training where the absolutely untrained girls remain for 18 months and complete their course with six months on the district. If they are trained nurses they do six months at Gate Burton and six months on the district.

In lovely surroundings it would be impossible to leave without talking to one of the oldest retainers on the estate - that gallant old man with the grey beard and twinkling eyes, Mr Creed, the head gardener, who tends his fruit and vegetables as tenderly as the babies are tended. For he has grown up with some of his fruit trees in the 44 years of his service on the estate.

Car Rally at Gate Burton Hall
A car rally was held at Gate Burton Hall shortly

before the First World War. The photograph below shows a meeting of the Lincolnshire Automobile Club which was a flourishing concern among the pioneer motorists of the day. A number of open tourers and landaulets can be seen parked - eleven in all - as the owners roam the grounds at their ease. The local policeman stands at the foot of the flagpole on a sunny peaceful day, reflecting a way of life soon to be lost in the holocaust of the war.

Local resident Gillian Worrell remembers how Gate Burton had its own branch of the *Women's Institute* when Mrs Sandars resided at the hall. They held their meetings in the flower room, later called the WI room. Unfortunately, it had to be disbanded when Mrs Sandars left Gate Burton Hall as they could not find a suitable meeting house owing to the stipulation that meetings could not be conducted in someone's home.

Car rally in the grounds of Gate Burton Hall shortly before the First World War

St Helen's Church

The church at Gate Burton is dedicated to St Helen, mother of Constantine the Great, the first Roman emperor to make a law giving people freedom to worship as they please.

There have been three churches at Gate Burton, with very little known about the first. The list of rectors (which can be seen in the church porch) dates from 1219, with Roger de Caen as the first. This leads one to think that the first church would have been built in the early part of the thirteenth century, and probably in a Norman style of architecture, though there is no actual proof, unfortunately.

About 560 years later a petition signed by the lord of the manor, the rector and the churchwardens was sent to the ecclesiastical authorities. In it was stated that "...the ancient church at Gate Burton" was in such a dilapidated condition that it was no longer to be used for divine worship and that it was impossible

St Helen's Church, Gate Burton

for it to be repaired. Application was therefore made for permission to pull it down and build a new one. A faculty for this was granted in 1784.

In the reference room at the Lincoln city library there is a picture by J. C. Nattes, dated 1793, entitled 'Gate Burton Church', so this would be a picture of the second church. It shows a very plain structure in Georgian style more suggestive of a village meeting house than a church, as there does not appear to be any chancel, tower, spire or belfry.

In 1865 another petition was presented to the authorities asking for permission to rebuild the second church, and William Hutton, Lord of the Manor of Gate Burton and of the adjoining village of Knaith at that time, undertook to use as much material as possible from the previous church, to sell such material as could not be used and to put the money so obtained towards rebuilding and to supply from his own purse any further money which was needed.

He also promised that the new church would be erected as nearly as possible on the same foundations and that any monumental tablets, tombstones or coffins be replaced as close as possible to the positions previously occupied. The cost of the rebuilding was estimated by George Gilbert Scott, an experienced architect, as £1200.

A faculty was granted in 1866 and a contract was made with the builder, William Huddlestone, to

The oak organ gallery installed in 1926

do the work. This church is the one still in use today. It is built of stone lined with brick in modern Gothic style. Originally it consisted of a chancel, nave and square tower with three swinging steel bells. Three static bells were added during the incumbency of the Revered P. J. Hulbert (1990-1920).

Extensive alterations were made to the exterior of the church in 1926. An organ gallery, made from oak grown on the Gate Burton estate, was erected at the west end of the church.

The organ, which had been sited near the entrance to the vestry, was taken out, completely overhauled and an electrical mechanism installed. The entire chancel was redesigned with new altar, triptych and stone flooring. All this was done at a cost of £1415.00 by members of the Sandars family as a memorial to Mr

View from the gallery showing the 1926 renovation

J. D. Sandars who died in 1922. At the same time a complete set of silver gilt altar furnishings was given, and the east end of the chancel was panelled in oak.

The new altar is one of the most beautiful in the district. The centre panel of the triptych has five niches, the middle one holding a cross and the two on each side being filled with gilded statues of St Hugh of Lincoln, St Francis of Assisi, St Bernard and St Aidan.

In 1950 a vestry screen, panelled and carved to match the chancel wall, was given by people connected in various ways with Gate Burton as an offering for peace and the safe return of so many villagers from the two World Wars.

In 1952 a carved oak pulpit was donated by Mr J. E. Sandars in memory of his sister, formerly Miss Rosemary Sandars, who died in 1950 following an accident in the hunting field.

A perusal of various registers, records and directories reveals many interesting pieces of information about the church: for instance, in 1598, the rector, Theodore Walpole, writing a report on the parish stated that he was a B.A., married, of good behaviour but no preacher. His curate, Thomas Wood, was not a graduate and was described as no preacher. He was paid an annual stipend of £6 13s 4d. The Patron of the Living at that time was Lord Willoughby of Parnham.

In 1606 the widow Mrs Anne Farmery was churchwarden: a woman in such a role was most unusual. There is a gap in the Bishop's Transcripts from 1627 to 1662. Then, in 1701 charges are shown: four shillings for a burial, two shillings and sixpence

(2s/6d) for a marriage and two shillings for a baptism. In a series of surveys made by two successive Bishops of Lincoln it is stated that in 1711 the rector was Richard Crichloe; he held services once each Sunday, Catechism in Lent and Communion four times a year.

In 1778 no baptisms, marriages or burials were recorded, and in the following year there was only one marriage.

In the Middle Ages, the Government, anxious to establish wool as the staple industry of England, made laws ordering that woollen cloth be used wherever possible. It is interesting to note that in 1783 Mrs Elizabeth Hutton, who lived at Gate Burton, was buried in a linen shroud instead of a woollen one, and for this a penalty of £5 had to be paid.

The above article is based on an original written by the late Mrs Hetty Torr.

Gate Burton Mill

This delightful view is of the once fine post mill. It stood near Sorts Hill Farm on the south side of the Willingham Road east of the railway line. It stood on a hill and open to the wind from all directions.

The combination of two different types of sail is similar to those to be seen on the restored post mill at Wrawby near Brigg, the last survivor of hundreds of post mills once at work in Lincolnshire. The lack of sailcloths on the older pair of sails and the poor condition of some of the canvas-covered shutters on the spring-related pair of sails would suggest that the mill had gone out of commission sometime before this photograph was taken.

The white painted buck had a two storied full width rear porch which housed the flour dresser. The tailpole by which the timber buck and sails could be turned manually into the eye of the wind can be seen above the rear steps. These steps were hinged at the top and the lower end could be raised clear of the ground by means of the lever (talthur) and connecting irons seen at the lower end of the tailpole. These heavily constructed steps also acted as a prop when the mill was working. The single storey brick roundhouse has a tiled roof and a cap mounted under the floor of the buck.

The mill was depicted on Armstrong's map 1786/8 but not on the 1886, 6 inch OS map. The mill appears to have been owned in conjunction with the tower mill at Marton for a long period in the 19th century.

Gate Burton Mill

The Château

The Château was built in 1747-8 for a prosperous lawyer from Gainsborough named Thomas Hutton. Mr Hutton and his father before him had looked after the local business affairs of the Earl of Abingdon, who owned two small estates at nearby Gate Burton and Knaith, which had come into his family through an earlier marriage and were some distance from the rest of his very large property.

In 1744 the Earl was advised to sell the two estates and Hutton, seeing the chance of a bargain, purchased that of Gate Burton. (The neighbouring Knaith estate was sold to a Mr Dalton, and in the early 19th century Hutton's grandson bought it and brought it back to the Hutton family.) Gate Burton at that time had no hall or manor house, and rather than go to the expense of providing one Mr Hutton built the 'Château' on its wooded knoll above the river, with its garden and plantations around it, as a weekend cottage. There, according to his son, 'he could retire from the business of his office at Gainsborough, from a Saturday evening until the Monday morning'. He would have had his rooms on the first floor, with a kitchen and servant's room below.

The architect of the Château was John Platt, and it must have been almost his first work, designed when he was only 19. Platt came from a family of mason architects and for 50 years and more he practised as a builder and statuary mason as well as architect, all with equal success. He worked almost exclusively in Yorkshire; the Château is almost his only building outside the county. His many works include Mount Pleasant near Sheffield, Thundercliffe Grange in Eccles Field; and Page Hall, Eccleshall. He added a wing to Tong Hall; designed a fireplace replace for Renishaw; and staircases, made of marble from his own quarries, for Aston Hall and Clifton Hall.

Thomas Hutton finally began to build Gate Burton Hall in about 1765, and it was mostly complete by 1768. The Château came to be used simply as a summer house, an agreeable destination for picnics or the odd night 'in rural seclusion'. Towards the end of the century, however, alterations were carried out, including the addition of balconies at either end of the building. In the 19th century new windows were inserted, but they were on the wrong scale, being two panes wide instead of three; the exterior, above the rustication, was rendered and the roof was renewed.

In 1907 the Hutton family sold both Gate Burton and Knaith to the Sandars family, wealthy maltsters from Gainsborough. In the sale particulars the Château is described as a shooting box, so the upper floor

The Chateau pre-restoration

had probably been kept for the use of the family for shooting lunches and other such entertainments. After the war it was not lived in again, and it was left stranded without natural users. Gate Burton Hall, with its park, was sold again in 1974, but the strip of land along the river, where the Château stands, was retained and became part of the Knaith Hall estate, which had been inherited by a connection of the Sandars family.

The work of neglect and natural decay inevitably continued, accelerated as so often by the activities of vandals, until the building was approaching the point of collapse. In 1982 the owner, concerned for its survival but unable to afford the cost of repair himself, offered it to the Landmark Trust.

When the Landmark Trust took on the Château in 1982, there was little of the building that did not need extensive repair. Under the architect Philip Jebb, an old friend of the Trust, the builders Simons of Lincoln began work by dismantling anything

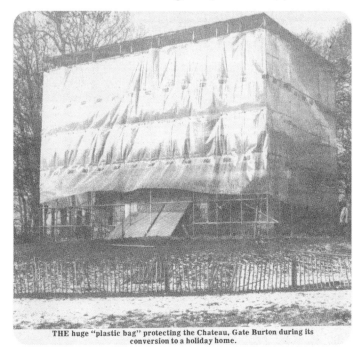

THE huge "plastic bag" protecting the Chateau, Gate Burton during its conversion to a holiday home.

Chateau during restoration in 1983

Chateau post-restoration in 1983

that was unsafe or past repair, and securing what remained. So the small balconies at either end, and the steps leading up on the west side, were taken down. The urns on the parapet, together with some fragments found lying around the building, were sent away for restoration. The parapet itself had also to be taken down, since the brickwork was unsafe. Beneath this, the entablature was also fairly insecure above the openings between the main block and the side wings, and had to be propped up from inside the building. The slates were taken off the roof, so that the condition of the timbers could be judged, and the decayed render hacked off the walls. Inside, what little remained was very rotten; after recording the mouldings, this too was hacked out.

At this point reconstruction could begin. Under the render, fair face pointing was found to the brickwork, indicating that the building had originally been plain brick above the rustication. So after the repair of structural weaknesses (in the niches on the end walls, for example), the brickwork was simply washed and repointed using lime putty. The stone rustication was treated similarly. Elsewhere, stone was renewed only where it was badly weathered, or where a section was missing, as in the balustrade of the central window. All the new work was carried out in Ancaster stone, which matched the original.

The roof timbers were nearly all unsound, so a new roof structure was needed. Enough of the original slates survived intact to cover the back and inner slopes of the side wings and elsewhere a new slate called Corunna Grey was used. The parapets were

rebuilt, incorporating lead water chutes, with new coping stones where necessary. The chimney was also rebuilt as closely as possible to the original in John Platt's drawing, which is in the Sheffield City Library. The balconies were not replaced, however; they were almost certainly later additions, and since an internal staircase would have to be built anyway they were not needed for access. The two doorways leading to them have therefore become windows.

All the windows needed replacing, which has given the opportunity to return to the original proportions of three panes, which suits the scale of the building much better.

The work to the exterior was completed by the return of the urns to the corners of the parapets. Only two had proved to be beyond repair, and to replace these matching new urns were carved.

Inside the building just about everything is new work. Only the first-floor fireplace and some paving stones on the ground are from the building as it was. Since the plasterwork seemed to be later than 1747, however, it was not replaced with an exact copy but with mouldings more typical of the mid-18th century. A staircase was fitted into one wing, bedrooms into the other, and the kitchen and bathroom on the ground floor. The Château was ready once more for its original purpose as a place of retirement from business, for a weekend or longer, and can now be rented all year round by up to two people through the Landmark Trust.

GATE BURTON IN THE NEWS

A newspaper story dated 9 January 1976 following the great storm:

'Gainsborough was one of the worst hit areas in the country in Friday's gale. Although thousands of pounds' worth of damage was caused no-one was killed or seriously hurt.

A Gate Burton couple had a miraculous escape when Friday's hurricane winds blew a giant elm tree on to their cottage. Charles Scott 56 and his wife Nora 67 had been in bed for only about ten minutes when the tree crashed

through the roof of the bedroom killing their nine year old dachshund, Floppy. The little dog had been lying at the foot of the bed when it was killed by the falling masonry and timber.

'It was terrifying, we heard this roar and crack and then it was all on top of us', Mrs Scott told The News. The Scotts had gone to bed at about 11.15pm, leaving a fire burning in the grate in the living room. About ten minutes later the huge elm tree crashed down on the cottage and the roof collapsed on top of them.'

GATE BURTON IN PICTURES

An early drawing of Gate Burton Hall

Earlier photo of Gate Burton Hall covered in ivy

Early farming at Gate Burton

A group of children from Gate Burton school at the West Lindsey Musical Festival in 1938.

Back row, stood left to right: Colin Fenwick (Knaith), Barbara Talbot (Knaith Hill), Unknown, John Justin's sister, Wing (Hetty?), Pam Denby (Gate Burton), Harry Carr (Knaith Hill), Unknown, Bill Cheetham (Knaith Hill), Dennis Fenwick (Knaith), Harry Fisher (Marton).

Seated in front row, left to right: Unknown, Unknown, Unknown, Edward Cheetham (Knaith Hill).

Gate Burton Hunt 1830 by John E Ferneley 1782-1860

Gate to Kettlethorpe Hall

KETTLETHORPE

Kettlethorpe is a village and parish in the vale of the River Trent, ten miles west of Lincoln and nine miles south of Gainsborough. The Fossdyke Canal passes just north of the parish and the River Trent forms the western boundary. Torksey parish is to the north and Newton on Trent parish to the south.

Introduction

Kettlethorpe was originally a Danish settlement dating from the 9th century, its name is said to derive from the thorpe or hamlet of *Ketil*, a Dane, who at some time made it his home, situated between the already existing villages of Laughterton and Fenton. (Kettlethorpe is not mentioned in Domesday Book of 1086 - although nearby Newton on Trent is, for example - and is not seen in historical documents until 1220.) Coincidentally, Ketil's countryman, Torkil, was resident in about 870 at a nearby important inland port to which he was to give his name, Torksey.

Kettlethorpe village has just 13 homes and 55 people, says its website, and it takes just minutes to walk from one end to the other, but although small it is perfectly formed.

There is the church of St Peter and St Paul at the centre. I mean this both literally and metaphorically, since the church is a vital focal point for the community and anyone attending its traditional Sunday morning services will enjoy a friendly welcome and fresh cup of tea at its conclusion. It's really the place to be if you need to renew acquaintances and catch up on the latest village news.

To the north of the churchyard there is a kissing gate exit to an avenue of lime trees leading towards an old rectory, the trees having once framed the rector's route to church and back.

Nearby is the village hall, originally built in 1854 as a Sunday school. Frank Gourley, father of well-known local farmer Ian, bought the village hall after it had not sold at auction and rented it to the village for the nominal sum of £1 a year. Ian was to bequeath it to the village in 1960 in memory of his parents. The village hall is now used regularly for Women's Institute, parish council and other social activities, as well as for private parties.

South of the church stands the imposing and largely Victorian pile that is Kettlethorpe Hall, focal point for much of the history of the village.

The whole scene is complemented by some period country homes and gardens to the west and, to the east, a gentle swell in the landscape applies the finishing touch to this 'romantic spot embowered by trees', says Thorold, and that's a fair visual description of this village with a unique and important history.

VILLAGE TALES

Kettlethorpe Hall

It was Sir Hugh Swynford (c.1340-1371), Lord of the manors of Kettlethorpe and Coleby, who established Kettlethorpe's place in history. He married Katherine de Roët (pronounced Roay), from Hainault, who later became mistress and then wife of John of Gaunt, Duke of Lancaster and third son of Edward III.

John married Katherine in 1396, an unpopular union and a remarkable demonstration of love in the days of dynastic marriages. The historical novel *Katherine* by

Anya Seton, which became widely popular following its publication in 1954, was inspired by this story and this novel in turn inspired popular historian Alison Weir to write in 2007 a more bare-factual account entitled *Katherine Swynford*.

Katherine's sister, Philippa, was wife of the famous English poet, Geoffrey Chaucer. Katherine's four children by John of Gaunt were eventually legitimised under the name of Beaufort. Katherine appears to have been regarded with respect by both Richard II

Kettlethorpe Hall, as depicted on the Ordnance Survey 6" map, 1885

(John of Gaunt's nephew) and Henry IV (his son). In 1383 Richard granted her the right to enclose a deer park of 300 acres within her manor of Kettlethorpe, which survived until 1830. But it was a strict term of the legitimation of her children that neither they nor their heirs should ever lay claim to the throne.

This condition was simply ignored by Henry VII, whose mother was Lady Margaret Beaufort, great-granddaughter of Katherine and John and Henry's only claim to be in direct line of descent.

Katherine died in 1403 and was buried in Lincoln Cathedral but the Swynford line continued at Kettlethorpe until the late 15th century. Only the gateway, some of the walls of the manor tower, parts of the moat and cellar remain from this time.

A Local Skirmish
Charles Hall was owner of the hall in the early 17th century and it was to remain in his family for three generations, spanning some 120 years. It was during his time, on 26 July 1645, during the English Civil War, that a skirmish took place at Kettlethorpe at which (according to Roundhead accounts) the Royalists were routed, suffering four casualties and being chased to within three miles of Newark.

Charles was returned to the Commonwealth Parliament in 1654. The brick walls surrounding the garden date from this period, and his arms feature on one of the gate pillars - a talbot's head (a talbot was a

medieval hunting dog) and the initials CH.

In the 18th century, Kettlethorpe passed from the Hall to the Amcotts family, whose arms are displayed over the house entrance. In this period Kettlethorpe became a very large house, and an obituary for Sir Wharton Amcotts MP in 1807 asserts that '...at no place was the old English hospitality kept up with greater spirit than at Kettlethorpe'. Shortly thereafter it fell into disrepair and the present house was reconstructed in the 1860s out of the old manor by Weston Cracroft-Amcotts (who represented mid-Lincolnshire in Parliament).

The house is something of a history lesson in miniature, with some remarkable features preserved. As well as the medieval gatehouse, stone walls and some curious carved heads, there is a small 17th century oak-panelled room, an early 18th century panelled dining room in the old tower and a fine marble fireplace. The drawing room has a particularly fine stuccoed ceiling from the end of the 18th century, while the library and front hall are Victorian.

To the Present
In the 1980s Kettlethorpe Hall passed back into the hands of a Parliamentarian, the Rt Hon Douglas Hogg. In the 1990s wife Sarah was conferred the title of Baroness Hogg of Kettlethorpe in recognition of her services at Downing Street. It is a curious coincidence that the Hogg family arms, like the Swynfords', consists of a shield bearing three boars' heads.

Acknowledgements
We are grateful to Douglas and Sarah Hogg for providing access to their home and for material on the history of the hall. The above account follows closely that written by Sarah in 2000, supplemented by a slim and authentically yellowed booklet from the library of Douglas, entitled The Manor and Rectory of Kettlethorpe by R E G Cole, Prebendary of Lincoln, being an extract from Vol 36 of Transactions of the Lincolnshire Archaeological Society, 1911.

Katherine Swynford

How on earth did the Lady of the manor of Kettlethorpe become so significant in English history and in the English (now British), royal family?

Basically she became the mistress and then third wife of John of Gaunt and bore him four illegitimate children; John, Henry, Thomas and Joan. Katherine and John were married in 1396 and their children were made legitimate by decree of the pope and King Richard II.

Lady Katherine is, therefore, the stepmother of Henry IV (who referred to her in her second widowhood as 'the King's Mother') - John and Katherine are the great-great-grandparents of Henry VII through their son John (Earl of Somerset). Henry VII founded the Tudor dynasty (which included Henry VIII and Elizabeth I) and became King after defeating Richard III at the Battle of Bosworth in the final stage of the Wars of the Roses. Katherine and John are great-great-great-grandparents of Henry VIII; great-great-great-great-grandparents of Elizabeth I. The Scottish House of Stuart is also descended from them through John the Earl of Somerset's daughter Joan, who married James I of Scotland - and the present Queen of the United Kingdom is descended from John and Katherine.

Born in Hainault in modern day Belgium, Katherine came to England with her father, Sir Paon de Roet, who was attached to the household of Philippa of Hainault, wife of King Edward III.

Nothing much is known of Hugh Swynford until his marriage to Katherine. It would seem that the marriage was arranged under the auspices of Queen Philippa of Hainault and was not to Katherine's liking. Unusually, they did not remain at court after their marriage. It would appear that Hugh offended someone, the registers state that he was sent back to Kettlethorpe to wait the time when and if his services as a fighter should be required!

Hugh had left home at about the age of 15 to join up Edward III's army which was invading Scotland. During this period he first met John of Gaunt, then Earl of Richmond, and they appear to have established some rapport.

Hugh then appears again fighting for the Black Prince at Poitiers, it would seem to be at this time that Hugh was knighted and returned home. Hugh then goes to London, with squire in tow to do knights' service to the Duke of Lancaster, his feudal overlord. Hugh owned a manor at Coleby that belonged to John's manor of Richmond.

He does not appear to have had much time for chivalry and earthly pursuits. However, he was a 'damn good soldier' and is described in the registers as 'a shrewd and terrifying fighter'.

It would seem that this exile was short-lived, however, just long enough for him to collect his rents, sort

out manor affairs, settle Katherine into her new home and depart in August 1366 for Aquitaine. John of Gaunt and Edward, the Black Prince, were entering into war in Castile with King Pedro against his brother *Henry of Trastámara*, who had usurped the throne.

John of Gaunt

Katherine was with child when he left and Hugh obviously confided this fact to John. Again, the registers record that Katherine was escorted to Bolingbroke to spend Christmas and New Year with Duchess Blanche who was herself with child.

Hugh was sent back to Lincoln shortly after having taken part in the battle of Najera and distinguishing himself again as a good warrior and battle tactician. No more is heard of either Hugh or Katherine until 1369 by which time they had a son, named Thomas after his grandfather.

Hugh and Katherine's relationship had mellowed, but Katherine appears to have been quite pleased to go to Bolingbroke to wait on the Duchess Blanche. Sadly, by the time she arrived, Blanche was dying of plague. Katherine nursed her and was able to locate a priest to give her the last rights. It would then appear that Hugh sanctioned Katherine's journey to London in Blanche's funeral train.

Quite what happened when she got to London is not really certain, but Katherine returned to Kettlethorpe as an armiger (a person entitled to use a coat of arms)

'John Wycliffe reading his translation of the Bible to John of Gaunt' Brown, Ford Madox - 1847. Here we see John of Gaunt and Katherine as the woman in white in the background with a child on her knee, probably her eldest son John.

as an armiger (a person entitled to use a coat of arms) in her own right. Her blazon was designed, bestowed and registered by John of Gaunt. He also rewarded her, as a pension, 'all issues from, and profits from his towns of Waddington and Wellingore to be paid yearly'. Hugh was, not unnaturally, not too happy, but seems to have accepted the reason for the gift. This was 'for the care shown to the late Duchess and for the Lancastrian children after their mother's death'.

It is known that John and Katherine disappeared for several weeks prior to his second marriage, and presumably this is when she became his mistress. She returned to England and was obviously pregnant because she gave birth to John, later John Beaufort. It was assumed that John was Hugh's posthumous child (Hugh by this time having died of wounds in Bordeaux), but when Henry was born to John and Katherine, they acknowledged him as their son.

Cracroft-Amcotts and the Disposal of their Kettlethorpe Estate

Major Frederick Augustus Cracroft-Amcotts inherited the estate in about 1883 after the death of his father, Weston Cracroft-Amcotts. He married Emily Grace Willson in 1885.

The family had owned Kettlethorpe for some time and had been active builders in the village. The village hall was initially built as a Church of England Sunday school in 1854, the rectory in 1856, the hall rebuilt in 1863 and Hall Farm in 1895. Several schemes were made for restoring and rebuilding the church between 1809 and 1877.

Frederick died in 1898 aged 44 in a riding accident. A subscription was raised in his memory and from this a new church organ was bought and the lychgate was built, his initials are on the inside of it. His widow continued to run the estate until her death in 1936.

Their son, Weston Cracroft-Amcotts had inherited the Hackthorn estate and decided to put his energy into its management and so the sale of the

Kettlethorpe Estate started. In May 1942 74 lots of houses and land totalling 1167 acres were auctioned by John D. Wood of London at Lincoln. The majority were tenanted and prices varied. Some lots were sold prior to auction, others were withdrawn as not reaching their reserve. Houses were selling for £100-£400 including large gardens. Land made £4-£20 acre with the higher figure including house and buildings. Wages at this time would be £2-£4 a week.

Soon after this auction 18 lots that had not sold were put on the market again. It is not known what the result of this was.

In February 1949 Park Farm with 360 acres and 65 acres of nearby woodland were auctioned by Knights of London at Lincoln

In October 1949 Ivy Cottage and Keepers Cottage were auctioned by Tinsley and Laverack of Lincoln. In July 1960 Lodge Farm (182 acres), Church Farm (128 acres), Hall Farm (357 acres) and two fields were auctioned by John D Wood.

Kettlethorpe Church

The church of Saint Peter & Saint Paul serves the parishes of Fenton, Kettlethorpe and Laughterton.

Built in 1809, it was described by William White in *The Lincolnshire History and Directory* of 1872 as the white church, because it was built of cream brick. There has been a place of worship on the site since

the 12th century and the original church features in a painting by Claude Nattes of 1793, a copy of which hangs in the church. The first recorded rector was a Richard de Keal in 1220.

An application was made by Rector Charles Massingberd and the churchwarden Edward Waddington in 1808 to demolish the by then dilapidated church and rebuild on the same site. The cost was to be met by Lady Ingilby-Amcotts of Kettlethorpe Hall, with the proviso that 'the selling of lead and other useless materials' be set against it. In commemoration of the rebuild a coat of arms was painted by W P Pudsey of Gainsborough in 1812 and it hangs over the entrance.

Little remains of the old church - there is a 15th century stone corbel with a shield bearing the arms of France and England, and slabs in the south aisle commemorating the Hall family. The tower, part built of stone from the old church, has three bells: one a pre-Reformation treble, hung in about 1710, with the inscription *Sit nomen domini benedictum* (May the name of the Lord be blessed); the others a tenor and second bell, both dating from 1718.

A visiting archaeologist has suggested that a stone coffin (minus its lid) north of the churchyard may have been removed from the old church prior to demolition. It was common during the medieval age for deceased priests to be buried in such a coffin within the churchyard.

The church was enlarged in 1864 by adding a north aisle. This contains monuments and stained glass in memory of the Cole family who were connected to Fenton for over 300 years and who were stalwart members of the church. The latest additions are the grave marker and citation awarded to Major N W Wells-Cole, killed in action in 1918, and that of Thomasina, wife of Victor Henry Wells-Cole, who died 3 June, 2002, aged 102.

The pulpit has an interesting story. It was seen outside an antique shop in Brittany by Mrs Amcotts, in poor condition, covered in paint and stucco. She would buy it but only if it could be cleaned without damage. Mrs Amcotts left it with the dealer for a week and on return was amazed to find the pulpit fully restored and was told it had spent the week in a nearby river, with only the natural motion of the water having cleaned it.

There are many epitaphs around the church. One of particular charm is that of John Becke (rector, 1576–97), who left £4 pa for distribution to the parish poor:

I am a Becke or river as you know,
And wat'red here in ye Church, ye schole, ye pore, While God did make my springs here to ow:
But now my fountain stopt it runs no more:
from Church and schole mi life is now bereft
but to ye pore foure poundes I yearly le.

The chancel & window of St Peter and St Paul church, Kettlethorpe

The charity continues today under the title of *Kettlethorpe and District United Charities.*

The organ and lychgate were donated by the Friends of H A Amcotts, using money collected after his death in 1897. Although in need of some renovation the organ is ably played every week by Colin Kyme of Newton on Trent who has been church organist for over 30 years.

The year 2009 was special for the church, marking the bicentenary of its rebuilding, and was celebrated by a number of events, a highlight being a service of thanksgiving and rededication officiated at by Rt Rev John Saxbee, Bishop of Lincoln, during which a message of congratulation from the Queen was read out.

The churchyard has three items of particular interest to visitors: the stone coffin previously mentioned; a medieval cross which is defined in the *Ancient Monuments and Archaeological Areas Act of 1979* as being 'of national importance'; and an oak tree planted in 2003 to commemorate the 600th anniversary of the death of Katherine Swynford.

Kettlethorpe church has a regular flow of visitors from overseas who have made what they call the 'Katherine Trail'. There is a permanent exhibition of the story in the church and a genealogical chart hangs in the porch showing how the present royal family is descended from the union of John and Katherine.

Rita Atkin, Laughterton
(With acknowledgement to Trevor Richmond of Kettlethorpe, who provided much of the source information.)

 Kettlethorpe Church, Fred Dixon

The WI Rally at Kettlethorpe Hall

In 1934 Mrs E G Cracroft-Amcotts was president of the *Lindsey Federation of Women's Institutes*. It was on Wednesday 6 June of that year that the annual rally of the WI was for the first time held at her home, Kettlethorpe Hall. (Incidentally, the Kettlethorpe estate had been in the Amcotts family since 1743.) The rally was deemed a notable success, as a local paper gushingly reports:

'Mrs Amcotts opened her heart as well as her home and her invitation to pick a bunch of flowers was symbolic of the thoughtful preparations for the comfort of her one thousand five hundred guests which she had been making for months beforehand. Kettlethorpe itself is one of those rare places which seem to reflect and enhance the charm of their owners and the fresh green lawns and rhododendrons glowing against the fine old trees were hosts in themselves. A Rally in such surroundings and with such a hostess must be a source of pleasure and inspiration to every Institute member.'

Not to be outdone, another paper reported that the total in attendance was nearly three thousand - though either total is impressive - and bore this quote from Mrs Amcotts, including the parenthetic 'laughter':

'May I express my hearty thanks to you all for having come from all over Lindsey to honour us at Kettlethorpe Hall. We should have liked a little more sunshine but we are very thankful that those who came from the east and north left the rain behind them, and we shall be thankful for it tonight (laughter).'

There were tents containing handicrafts and produce and these were judged rather seriously as Mrs Amcotts relates:

'Mr Murray was especially pleased with the bottled fruits and said there was a greater variety. When he first judged there were 36% turned out but this year only 1% were not correctly sealed ...' and later 'We did not receive quite so complimentary comments on the dairy section. The judge thought we were poor butter makers, and it is up to us all next time to make it better. There must be no buttermilk and no salt.' Quite right, Mrs A!

The event had some quaint features which WI members of today may care to note. There was apparently an orchestra; a Dr Gordon Slater, organist at Lincoln Cathedral, adjudicated a singing festival in the village hall, there was 'massed singing in the Hall gardens' and a 'programme of mime' was given by a number of WI groups, one of them entitled 'Miss 1834 and Miss 1934', while in the evening there were two performances of 'living whist' staged by members of the Kettlethorpe Institute and friends. Make of that what you will.

MY STORY

Ian Gourley

Ian was born in Lincoln in August 1934 as Thomas Ian Gourley. At the time his parents were living where he lived at Hall Farm, Kettlethorpe. His great-grandfather, John, came to Kettlethorpe in 1880 as tenant on the farm which was then known as Avenue Farm after the avenue of elm trees that ran from the farm to Kettlethorpe Hall, where he lived. (Sadly, the trees were victims of the Dutch elm disease outbreak in the 1970s and have not been replaced despite an early attempt by Ian to do so.) In 1895 the Cracroft-Amcotts family wanted to move back into the hall and they built a house for John at what is known today as Hall Farm.

John's son, Thomas, took over running the farm in 1895. Thomas had six children: four boys (one of whom died in infancy) and two girls. Two of the boys, Frank and Henry, inherited the farm in 1931. Some time later Henry moved onto another farm, leaving Frank to run Hall Farm. Frank's wife was a Wilmot, Kate, from Newton, and in 1934 they had their only child, Ian, the subject of this article. During 1940-5 Ian attended Kettlethorpe School, Laughterton, and then went on to Gainsborough Grammar School.

In 1942 Frank, in expanding his holding, bought Village Farm, Laughterton, which has since been known as Home Farm and is now a private property. In 1960 Frank bought the freehold of Hall Farm in partnership with son, Ian. It was a shrewd purchase, as Ian described: *"We had the chance before the auction of the property to buy it and, with an understanding bank manager and the pooling of our funds, we bought it at a very good price, an action we've never regretted."*

Ian met a young lady called Margaret Laird at Collingham Young Farmers and they married in 1967. They had twin daughters Helen and Joanne in 1969, followed by Alison in 1972. Both daughters Joanne and Alison have married farmers, one settling near Collingham and the other near Norwich, and Helen married a businessman. The Gourleys now have seven granddaughters.

"There have been vast changes in farming since I took over, I once recalled. We once had sixteen people working on the farm and with the rapid advance in technology that came down to four." said Ian. "Where once we had horses drawing carts and stacked corn in sheaves we now have the job done by one man sat in the cab of a giant machine."

Ian was an active member of the community and in spring of 1973 he became one of the founding councillors of Kettlethorpe Parish Council. For the next 28 years he was to serve in various roles, including being the first chairman. Ian's father, Frank, had bought Kettlethorpe village hall when it had not sold at auction. He then let it to the village for £1 a year. Later, in 1975, Ian gave the hall to the village in memory of his parents.

Ian was also chairman of the Magnificent Seven, who got the memorial erected in 1994 on the triangle at Laughterton to the two aircrews that crashed locally during the war, a Stirling bomber at Park Farm and a Lancaster bomber on the Laughterton marshes where there was a practice bombing range.

Ian won a first at the Lincolnshire Show for three years in succession with his pedigree Charolais cattle. Some of his happiest memories of farming were taking stock to Gainsborough market, when 40 butchers and five wholesalers would be bidding.

Ian sadly passed away on November 11th 2011.

KETTLETHORPE IN PICTURES

Kettlethorpe Hall often hosted the local fete, here we can see children in fancy dress and dancing around the maypole

An early hunt at Kettlethorpe

Kettlethorpe WI group

The programme of events for the WI Rally in 1934

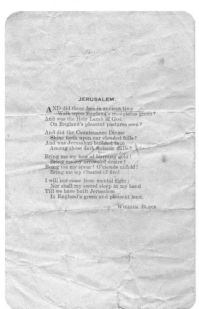

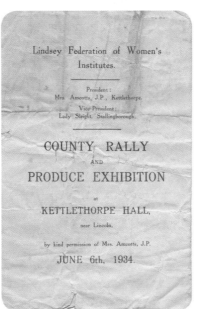

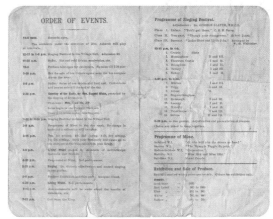

 Fenton residents parading outside Kettlethorpe village hall

 Kettlethorpe Sunday school in 1956

Mr Espen, former churchwarden of St Mary's

KNAITH

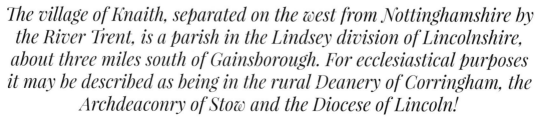

The village of Knaith, separated on the west from Nottinghamshire by the River Trent, is a parish in the Lindsey division of Lincolnshire, about three miles south of Gainsborough. For ecclesiastical purposes it may be described as being in the rural Deanery of Corringham, the Archdeaconry of Stow and the Diocese of Lincoln!

Introduction

The village stands at a bend in the River Trent, and this may account for its name which in its first spelling appears to be derived from two Scandinavian words meaning 'neck' and 'knee', thus describing a knee-shaped neck of land. Ekwall gives the derivation as meaning 'the landing place by the knee or bend', i.e. of the Trent.

The view of the Trent valley at this point was described by the 18th century writer Arthur Young in his survey of Lincolnshire published in 1799: '*There are very agreeable scenes from the plantation of Knaith, the winding of the Trent and the rich plains of meadow, alive with cattle, are features of a very agreeable country.*' This might still partly describe the view of Knaith from the Nottinghamshire side but the scene in that county has been much changed in recent years following erection of the West Burton power station.

Knaith is entered in the Domesday Book (the great survey of England commissioned by William the Conqueror in 1086) under its first name of Cheneide. It then went on to be referred to as Kneia in 1199, Cheie in 1223, followed by Knayth, until it finally arrived at Knaith.

Knaith has been the scene of some dramas: in 204 AD the Trent overflowed for some miles on each side and drowned hundreds of people. Much later, in Cromwell's time, Knaith was the scene of battle and a number of spearheads, battle-axes and skeletons have recently been dug out of Knaith's soil.

Interestingly, the first holder of land in Knaith (under the new feudal system) was Remigius, a Benedictine monk and supporter of William the Conqueror who was present at the Battle of Hastings. Remigius began to build his cathedral at Lincoln in 1085 but died a few days prior to its consecration in 1092.

VILLAGE TALES

Church of St Mary

The present church is a small stone building in the late Decorated Period, formed from part of the nave of the convent church that once stood here. (The Decorated style is late 13th/early 14th century English Gothic, characterised by its window tracery, the east end of Lincoln Cathedral being an example.)

The convent closed in 1539 and for almost a century the building was left to decay but in 1630 a church was formed out of the remains of the convent chapel. The original building had a small tower and the building was roofed. The choir arch in part remains but is now blocked. The nave had originally five three-light windows, there being two on each side and one at the west end. Those on the south side are still perfect, retaining their elegant flowing tracery but which unfortunately are concealed from an interior view by the Georgian plaster ceiling put in to cover the roof beams.

The hand-carved medieval pew ends have survived and there are good examples of 17th century work in both the pulpit and the desk. The *baldacchino* (Italian for canopy) over the altar, erected during the Victorian restoration, is an uncommon feature for an English church.

An early drawing of the south side of St Mary's Church, a short stroll away from both Knaith Hall and the River Trent.

The architect J T Micklethwaite, writing of the church's restoration in 1894, described his first visit to the church: *'When I first visited it, in August 1892, the outside was so completely hidden by a dense growth of ivy that it looked more like an abandoned barn than a Christian church, and there was some difficulty in getting at it sufficiently to read the story...'*. He then goes on to describe the building and rebuilding of the past and of the pews he writes: *'they [pews] are evidently the work of the village carpenter - very solid and substantial, but also very rude'*, by which he means rudimentary. However, to us today, to see the human hand in the woodwork of a church is a considerable part of its charm.

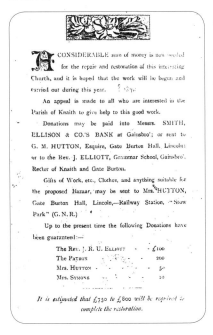

Fundraising effort is announced for restoration of the church in 1894. Donations can be made to Rev J Elliott (father of Miss D Elliott) and to Mr G Hutton of Gate Burton Hall, who in 1908 was to sell the hall to the Sandars family.

A Tale of Two Fonts

Until very recently, little was known about the history of the font in St Mary's, other than it was believed to date from the early 14th century and thought to resemble other designs such as the one in Bradley church near Grimsby. However, a chance discovery has unearthed information that another, almost identical baptismal font, exists in Australia, and that both fonts are extremely rare, the only two of this design known to exist, though they are separated by eleven thousand miles and a mere five centuries in time.

The mystery began to unravel when Mr Brian Corless, Hon Secretary and Archivist from St George's Church, Malvern, Victoria, Australia, was searching for more information about St George's font. He scanned Google images, entering 'church font imp heads', having previously searched the internet to no avail, and was immediately directed to St Mary's at Knaith with pictures of the interior and of course, the font. Mr Corless contacted Rev Phillip Wain, who contacted Eddy Overson, a keen delver of St Mary's history, and the ensuing communication between them revealed the extraordinary connection the

fonts have made between two churches situated on either side of the world.

The font at St George's was carved in situ by a William Egan in 1872 who was employed by John William Brown, a monumental mason in Melbourne, born in Kidderminster, Worcestershire 1832 who arrived in the Colony of Victoria c.1857 and lived into his ninety-third year. Mr Corless believed that the two fonts are so very much alike that William Egan must have been working from a clear pattern or model, but he couldn't think how that could have happened.

Eddy sent Mr Corless a copy of an engraving of the font in his possession, totally unaware that this was the key that would enable the mystery to be unlocked. Despite the lack of any note or explanation attached to the photocopy, and once again proving his considerable skill and tenacity in searching the internet, Mr Corless traced the original etching to a book entitled 'A Series of Ancient Baptismal Fonts' published in London in 1828. It includes a page 'Decorated English Fonts' and subtitled 'Knaith, Lincolnshire', with the following description:

'This very splendid font is we think altogether the handsomest we ever saw. The heads are admirably executed and all vary in design; in the deep hollow under the bowl is the ball flower.'

The book points out the rarity of this design: *'As the Decorated style was in use but little more than seventy years, very few fonts of that character are to be found, and of these some, though good in design, are very indifferent in execution.'*

Further investigation found that this book is in the catalogue of the State Library of Victoria, formerly the Melbourne Public Library, just a stroll down the road from the works of monumental mason John Brown, and ideally situated to be able to provide a source of inspiration and measurement for a skilful stonemason such as William Egan.

The engraving of St Mary's font from the book 'A Series of Ancient Baptismal Fonts' published in London in 1828 by Septimus Prowett

The delightful engraving and fulsome commendation included in the book surely persuaded the authorities to commission a copy of the font for their new church of St George.

The engraving was made by Robert Roberts and drawn by Francis Simpson Jr, a well-established antiquarian artist and archivist. He was, by the way, the long-time mayor of Stamford.

We are deeply indebted to Brian Corless and Eddy Overson for unearthing the amazing link between our baptismal fonts, one in England and the other in Australia!

The Early 14th Century Font of St Mary's Church, Knaith, Lincolnshire, England

This fine example of a rare English Decorated Period font is described in the publication 'A Series of Ancient Baptismal Fonts' as being *very splendid... altogether the handsomest we ever saw. The heads are admirably executed and all vary in design; in the deep hollow under the bowl is the ball flower.'*

The Decorated English style was in use for little more than 70 years, until about the end of the reign of Edward III in 1377.

A copy of this book was held in the Melbourne Public Library - now the State Library of Victoria. It is

Early 14th century font of St Mary's Church

believed that this book and the engraving it contained was used as the source, both of measurement and inspiration. This allowed stonemason William Egan to demonstrate his skill and craftsmanship as can be seen in the photograph, left.

The 19th Century Font of St George's Church, Malvern, Victoria, Australia

Carved in situ in 1872, this image reveals the extraordinary similarity to the font of St Mary's church, Knaith - despite the two fonts being separated by eleven thousand miles and five hundred years. It is believed that the fulsome commendation that accompanies the engraving: *"...this very splendid font is we think altogether the handsomest we ever saw"*, persuaded the authorities to commission this excellent copy for their new church.

19th century font of St George's Church

Knaith Hall

K naith Hall is situated on the bank of the River Trent and is perfectly situated to provide extensive and beautiful views of the surrounding countryside. It has been the residence of Mrs Hutton, Mr Dalton and, further back, of the Willoughbys and D'Arcys, families of great importance

A drawing of Knaith Hall in 1793, showing the long west front of the house with some if its original mullioned windows.

in the 13th and 14th centuries. John D'Arcy was the first 'Lord of Knayth' in 1299, beginning a long association of the family with the parish of Knaith.

The architectural history of the hall is uncertain. The windows were changed in the late Georgian period, a bay has been added, and black and white timbering was added in Victorian times. The house is believed to be much smaller than it was in the days of the Willoughbys and drawings of the house show changes to the windows and the porch.

Knaith Hall is not only interesting for its building but also for the surrounding ground, where there is historical evidence of past buildings, allotments and even a famed tree - the *Wollemi* pine - with a lineage dating back to the Jurassic era.

Pine Tree to the Dinosaurs

Knaith Hall has a remarkable tree that until recently was thought to have been extinct for two million years. Nicknamed the 'pinosaur' and dating back to the Jurassic era - the time of the dinosaurs - the Wollemi pine (*Wollemia nobilis*) was found thriving in an Australian canyon in 1994. The *Wollemi* was named after the national park where it was found in Australia's Blue Mountains. It is still rare and fewer than 100 exist naturally. The tree is usually multi-trunked and has a very distinctive bark, being dark brown with knobbly bits that resemble chocolate rice breakfast cereal. The *Wollemi* - which is strictly not a pine but a member of the family *Araucariaceae* - most closely resembles plants known only from fossils, although it is related to the monkey puzzle tree.

Wollemi pines are now widely available for sale in Britain, having been grown from imported seedlings following the discovery in Australia. The tree at Knaith is thriving despite the recent harsh winters and, provided they are protected from the wind, Wollemis are quite hardy, preferring dappled shade. When grown outdoors they can grow to more than 130ft and live for 1000 years.

A Victorian makeover – black and white timber cladding (unusual for Lincolnshire) – and to the right what Arthur Young in c1813 described as 'a greenhouse planted like a conservatory'.

The Fenwicks

eonard Fenwick came to Terrace House Farm, Knaith, in 1937 bringing his family of seven boys and one girl. His eldest boy was Walford, David's father, who stayed on at the farm in 1945 to continue as a farmer, while the rest of the family moved on to a farm in Beelby near Grimsby. Let's face it, the Fenwicks *are* farming.

David lived at Terrace House Farm for 21 years, married, and then moved to Corner House Farm, Knaith, for 28 years before moving to his current home at Central Park Farm, Knaith Park. "I haven't travelled much" says David, which can readily be confirmed following a quick look at the map: you come out of one farm, cross the road and there's the next, and the third and present farm is about a mile up Knaith Hill.

David is what you might expect of a man who's spent his life on the farm, being ruddy in countenance, sturdy in frame and with a ready humour. His son, John, lived in a neighbouring field, within sight of David and wife Anne, in a home couched in some beautiful Lincolnshire countryside. John was naturally enough also a farmer, a tireless bundle of energy, and was wedded only to his work.

David has a clear memory of the time when the cows were driven from Terrace House Farm up the A156 to the nearby field, something that was eventually abandoned because of the growing amount of traffic.

More recently he recalls that in the 1980s/90s Knaith went through a fallow period, when the population dwindled away, but the village has since revitalised,

Walford Fenwick with wife Kathleen and children David, Susan and baby Margery

Terrace House Farm, Knaith. The entrance gate to Knaith Hall estate is across the A156 road at bottom left, and Knaith Hill is the road across the top of the photo

...and on the opposite corner stands Corner House Farm (photo taken in the 1960s)

71

he suspects due to people moving into the catchment area of the well-respected Queen Elizabeth's High School at Gainsborough, and indeed there is much new or refurbished housing to be seen as you drive up Knaith Hill from the A156.

So David's family has been in the Knaith area for over 70 years and his hale and hearty constitution gives you the impression David could be there for many a year to come.

John Fenwick sadly passed away on 31st of August 2010 aged 34 years.

In this personalised OS map, Central Park Farm is shown in the centre as plot no. 88 of the Knaith Park estate

The Naughty Nuns of Knaith

Visitors to St Mary's Church at Knaith are always intrigued to discover that the church is part of the chapel of the Heynings Nunnery, one of seven priories of Cistercian nuns in Lincolnshire.

Heynings nunnery was founded sometime during 1135-1154 AD. Ancient documents refer to its poverty and the meagre endowments as being 'notoriously insufficient'. You would think that being so small and so poor, the priory might have been dissolved in 1536 when Henry VIII declared himself Supreme Head of the Church of England, but for some reason it was spared and continued until 1539 when it was surrendered by the prioress, a Joan Sandforde, and eleven nuns. In the 16th century eleven was considered a good number of nuns for an English convent.

I have often wondered about those nuns and the life they led. It's such a serene place at Knaith, close to the river, with magnificent views across the Trent valley. I could imagine them in single file, pious heads bent, gliding along the cloisters to prayers, living a sheltered spiritual life in this lovely place.

Then I came across a copy of a document from the archives in Lincoln which described a visitation - an official visit of inspection - on 7 April 1440 from William Alnwick, the Bishop of Lincoln. I must admit, I was astonished. So I did a bit more digging about Cistercian priories in Yorkshire and Lincolnshire which confirmed that the surprising behaviour of the nuns at Heynings was by no means uncommon, and

it was all down to a severe lack of money, boredom and a hankering for a bit of pleasure.

As I read the archive report, the nuns emerged as individuals, women in poverty trying to survive. But even so, it was an eye-opener for me. I tried to imagine the scene of the visitation, and most of what follows is fact, taken directly from the archives, with just a sprinkle of my imagination to bring it to life.

Picture the scene:

Bishop William sits at a desk in a large dark hall, the slit windows in the stone walls to the sides of him letting in a cold April breeze off the River Trent. He is corpulent, an imposing figure in robes and rings. He shuffles paper on the desk and gestures at the chaplain to open the heavy oak door. The prioress, Dame Joan Hothum, enters wearing her brown habit of undyed wool, a cowl and a black veil covering the forehead. She is followed by the sub-prioress Dame Isobel Burtone who, it is recorded, comes from the neighbouring village of Gate Burton. (Most of the nuns were gentlefolk, and as members of the local gentry of relatively high standing.)

The nuns file into the hall, about eight or ten, and behind them are four lay-sisters in their white veils, and following them, three secular serving women. They will all be called upon to speak. There were eight lay-brothers who carried out the heavy labour in the community of Heynings, but none was present for the visitation.

The prioress and sub-prioress stand before the bishop, who holds a large scroll in his hand. He rises from his chair and opens proceedings with a prayer, *'And the word of God is set before this text, and all the building framed together groweth to an holy temple in the Lord'.* He goes on for some time in this vein and at length utters an amen. *'Amen'* the nuns reply and bow their heads. The amens echo around the stone walls and high ceiling. Someone coughs.

The bishop bows his head, makes the sign of the cross in the air, and sits. He signals to the prioress and hands her a certificate which addresses the requirements of the visitation. Bishop William then invites all in turn, starting with the prioress, to speak openly and honestly of their concerns about the priory. He reminds them that he will listen and not comment until the end of the meeting, when he will make his injunctions.

Dame Joan, the prioress, was entirely at ease. A tall haughty woman she was secure in her position, knowing full well that the bishop's hands were tied, that any misdemeanours or irregularities were minor, and that he wanted a quick settlement so he could go and dine at the local village hostelry.

Dame Joan inclined her head. *'The nuns have access too often to the house of the Treasurer in Lincoln,'* says Dame Joan, *'abiding there sometimes for a week.'* Two of the nuns blush and look down at the floor while another, Dame Alice Portere, who has also spent time in Lincoln on two occasions, stares incredulously at the Dame.

Joan tightens her lips. She well knows that Dame Joan also visits the Treasurer and enjoys his hospitality.

'All things are well,' declared Dame Isobel Burtone, wriggling her itchy chilblained toes.

Dame Katherine Hoghue, a stout red-faced woman from Hough-on the-Hill says, *'Some of the nuns are somewhat sleepy and come late to Matins and other canonical hours. And the house is in debt because of the large repairs we have done within and without and because of the scarcity of corn for several years'.*

Dame Ellen Cotum inclines her head meekly and says, *'All things are well'.*

Dame Alice Portere clasps her hands together in the sleeves of her robe and takes a deep breath. *'The prioress does not exhibit the state of the house in common,'* she says, avoiding the stare of Dame Joan and looking directly at the Bishop, noticing his red swollen nose. She continues *'The prioress, when she makes corrections, for those whom she loves she passes*

over lightly, and those whom she holds not in favour she harshly punishes.' Dame Alice finds breathing difficult which is making her voice falter and sound whiny. She clears her throat and lifts her shoulders. *'The prioress reproaches her sisters, saying that if they say ought to the bishop, she will lay on them such penalties that they shall not easily bear them.'*

A gasp is heard from the sisters. At this, Dame Joan steps forward. *'I deny the second part of the article, and I also deny the first part of the article.'*

Dame Alice has regathered her faltering courage and continues *'The prioress encourages the secular serving women, whom she believes more than her sisters in their words, to scold the same her sisters, and for this cause, quarrels do spring up between her and her sisters.'*

Part of an illuminated manuscript (dating from 1290- 1300) illustrating life in the nunneries, the abbess shown far left with book and crozier

There is a silence. The sisters behind Dame Joan and Dame Alice exchange glances, raise their eyebrows at each other. Some think Dame Alice is courageous, while most think she is a fool to speak so. The serving women nudge each other and grin.

'And,' Dame Alice continues, *'the prioress fells thick trees when there is no need.'* Snorts of laughter come from behind her, which she tries to ignore.

Dame Joan smiles, shakes her head slightly, and then bows her head before addressing the bishop. *'My lord, I can assure you that I have caused no trees to be felled save for the manifest advantage and with the express consent of the convent.'* More merriment continues.

The bishop slaps the desk with his hand. *'Enough.'* He looks at the nuns. *'Who else will speak?'*

Dame Agnes Bokke says that all things are well. Dame Ellen Bryg (from Brigg in Lincolnshire) says that all things are well. Dame Katharine Benet says all things are well. Dame Constance Burnham says that all things are well.

Dame Alice then turns and faces her sisters, her face red, her eyes fearful. Is she to be the only one to speak up against the prioress? She walks back to her sisters. Dame Agnes Sutton holds her arm, nods gently at her, and then steps past. She is a small wiry woman.

Her eyes are blue like cornflowers, and sparkle when she laughs. She is not brave, but she can see injustice is happening here today.

'The infirmary is occupied by secular folk to the great disturbance of the sisters.' Her high voice is crystal clear, like a waterfall on the hillside.

'Let an injunction be made,' says the bishop to the chaplain, who starts to scribble.
'I pray,' says Dame Agnes, *'that the cloister doors may be shut and opened at the due hours, forasmuch as they stand open too late.'*

'Let an injunction be made,' says the bishop.

'The nuns do hold drinkings of evenings in the guest chamber, even after Compline, especially when their friends come to visit them.' Dame Agnes stands as still as a rock. Nothing is heard except the scratch of the chaplain's quill.

The bishop coughs. *'Let an injunction be made that such drinkings shall not take place.'*

Dame Agnes then bows and turns towards Dame Alice, ignoring the mutterings of the others, and the icy stare of the prioress Dame Joan.

The bishop stands. *'Having heard your concerns and reserved my power of corrections, I have made my injunctions which will be implemented in this place. I now dissolve this visitation.'* He said a long closing prayer and made the sign of the cross again. Then he follows Dame Joan down the stone flags and out into the bright April afternoon.

One can only guess at what happened afterwards to the brave Dames Alice and Agnes. From just these few pages of the archives you can imagine the jealousies, the scheming, and the back-biting that

A beautiful section of stained glass featuring a medieval nun that has clearly been afforded saintly status, as some were

went on. I suspect Dames Alice and Agnes were not so innocent either. I can see them sneaking out of the nunnery in search of light relief. In fact, there is one colourful example of such a transgression in the form of Isobel Benet, the 15th century treasuress of Catesby Priory.

On one occasion, Isobel slipped into town and spent the evening with Augustinian friars dancing, singing and playing the lute until midnight. Isobel was certainly a character, she had plenty to say against her prioress when the bishop of Lincoln visited Catesby in 1442. She claimed the prioress was prone to outbursts, incompetent and negligent, had engaged in a liaison or two, and even pawned the priory's jewels. Isobel herself was said to have given birth to a child, the result of an affair with William Smythe, one time chaplain of Catesby.

So there you have it. A brief glimpse into the real and harsh lives of the Cistercian nuns. I must say I have come to admire them, the feisty Nuns of Heynings.

Dutch Cottage

As you drive on the A156 through Knaith towards Gainsborough you may notice Dutch Cottage on the right, so called because of its Dutch gable end, which was added to prop up the cottage.

It is thought the cottage dates back to 1600-1630. It is rumoured to be the most northerly mud-and-stud property in Lincolnshire, and parts of the original

walls still exist. (Mud-and-stud is a building technique that is thought to have originated in Lincolnshire and implies a framed construction and walls filled with mud and clay.) After the effects of Mother Nature finally took their toll the brick walls were built up to reinforce the property and the gable end was added.

Dutch Cottage is situated by the A156 but, Phil Simon has been informed, originally there would have been a road lying some 100 yards or so to the east, probably coming from the Gate Burton estate. The newer A156 road intruded somewhat on the property and all of the building north of the fireplace has been removed, reducing the footprint of the cottage by about half.

 The Dutch gable end (facing the A156) with its stylish curves reminiscent of Delft and other famous Dutch cities in the 17th century.

Dutch Cottage, Knaith, with its distinctive gable end

Thomas Sutton and Charterhouse

Thomas Sutton was born at Knaith in 1532, most likely in a building near to the convent known as the manor house, built before Knaith Hall. He was baptised at St Mary's church. Little is known of his early life though in 1558, aged 26, he decided to become a professional soldier in command of the Berwick garrison. After 22 years he moved to London in 1580.

Sutton was a shrewd businessman, earning his wealth through the coal trade, property dealing and by being moneylender to the nobility, and he further added to his fortune by marrying a rich widow, Lady Elizabeth Dudley, in 1582. Their combined fortune made Sutton the richest commoner in England.

It had been in Sutton's mind to create some major charitable work and in 1611 he established a hospital on the site of his house off

THOMAS SUTTON FOUNDER OF CHARTERHOUSE BORN IN THIS PARISH OF KNAITH 1522 & CHRISTENED AT THIS FONT DIED 12TH DECEMBER 1611.

There be of them that have left a name behind them

Ecclesiasticus 44:8

A plaque in St Mary's church with the year of Sutton's birth given as 1522 (it was 1532).

75

Charterhouse Square, near the City of London, for 80 impoverished gentleman and a school for 40 poor boys.

Originally called the Hospital of King James in Charterhouse, it later became 'Sutton's Hospital in Charterhouse'. This was the origin of the famous Charterhouse School, one of the best known English public schools, which relocated to Godalming, Surrey, in 1872.

Thomas Sutton died on 12 December 1611 and left a great part of his fortune to Charterhouse. To commemorate that Knaith was Sutton's birthplace a plaque was erected in St Mary's church in 1951,

unveiled by General R A Hull, a former Governor of Charterhouse School.

Charterhouse Hospital engraved by Toms, c.1770

MY STORY

Alan Hardwick

I was born in Chesterfield, Derbyshire, the son of a coal miner, I grew up on Chesterfield Road and attended Netherthorpe Grammar School in the town. From a very early age I wanted to be a journalist, at that time in the area it was regarded as 'not a real job' but I was determined and I became a junior reporter for the local paper, The Derbyshire Times, and this is how I got the job...

I have been a lucky chap, and fate has intervened in my life on so many occasions to help me that if you wrote about it people wouldn't believe it. Whilst I was writing off for jobs I wanted to earn money and so I worked at a gentlemen's outfitters called Swallows, an upmarket shop in Chesterfield, where I was getting £5.00 a week. I had to wear a suit which was something I had never owned in my life, but the firm provided one as long as I paid 10 shillings and sixpence a week, so my take-home pay was greatly reduced.

I worked in the men's outfitters measuring for suits and shirts which were handmade at the time. It was a really old-fashioned shop like on 'Are you Being Served' with Mr Grayson, it was a wonderful experience. Unbeknown to me one of the people I worked with, a gentleman called Vincent Cleary who was a wonderful Irish gentlemen and very proud of his initials VC (and he ate polo mints all the time!), had a very good relationship with Jack Sanderson, the news

editor of the Derbyshire Times. Jack used to come to be measured for suits which means they come in on a regular basis so you form quite a good relationship with them. Vincent knew about my desire to be a journalist and he told me that he'd had a word with Jack Sanderson and that Jack wanted to see me, so instead of going home that night I walked across the road to the offices of The Derbyshire Times to be interviewed by Jack, a man who passed away a long time ago and a man for whom I had the deepest respect. Obviously he was a very good judge of character and he offered me a job.

From then on I became a junior reporter and built a career in newspapers until I transferred to television in 1973. I worked in newspapers all over in the southeast and southwest, but I am a northerner and always hankered after coming back to this part of the world. In 1973 (and here is another instance of fate) I had moved from Kent to Scarborough to cover the evening news where I was a subeditor and also part-time sports reporter. The reason I volunteered to do the sports reporting job was because reporting on the local rugby team in Scarborough on a Saturday meant that you got a half day off in the week, which I thought was a really good trade-off.

One of the friends I made was a rugby player called John Mead who was a journalist at that time for

Yorkshire Television, so we had something in common but it really didn't mean that much to me. One day I was working in the office when it was a 'page change', because we were a daily newspaper, for the different editions you had to do a page change, it was a technical thing and I was the only person who could do it as it was a sports page and at that time I was a sports reporter and editor. John Mead phoned me and said that we needed to cover a story at Butlin's in Filey, they had a film crew coming over from Hull but because of the sea fret (a seaside fog) they couldn't land the helicopter with the reporter. I used to travel in helicopters frequently, Yorkshire Television had two at one time, so John asked if we could go over and cover the reporting. I explained that I would love to but I still had to cover the page change as I was the only one who could do it, so I said I would get someone else to cover the reporting at Butlin's. I asked around and everybody was so busy despite the fact this was for Yorkshire Television who paid very well in those days. I was still very keen to cover this story myself and just when I thought it was never going to happen, and this is the truth, but the truth is often stranger than fiction, a man called Barry Hampshire walked into the office. It was Barry's day off but he was the only other person who could do the page change and so I asked him if he could do this interview at Butlin's in Filey, he said he couldn't but he could take over from me if I wanted to go and do it.

So I set off to Butlin's in Filey and met this news crew, who at the time seemed very intimidating but we went on to become very good friends. There was a camera man, an electrician and a sound recorder and they said "Do your journalist bit and ask the questions and we will do the rest". That night I got a name check on Calendar Television and I was worried that I would lose my job as, although it was all official, not cash in hand or anything, I had omitted to tell my boss. So the next morning I went into the office with a little bit of trepidation to be met with the warmest praise, "We saw you on television last night, you were really good," and Yorkshire Television liked what they saw and offered me a job.

That was 1973 and I worked for Yorkshire Television for 30 years. That that is how fate has intervened in my life. Once you are a journalist you are always a journalist and I got to meet incredible people and got to do incredible things. I have flown in everything there is to fly in except a space rocket, I have flown in helicopters and old biplanes. I have driven lots of different vehicles including the James Bond Aston Martin from the original film, in fact I was in Harewood Park outside Leeds and I was behind the wheel of the Aston Martin when the man who owned it said I could take it out for a drive. Harewood House is just opposite some very grand homes with drive-in-and-out driveways so I was belting along and I swung into a driveway narrowly missing a car containing Lord Harewood and Lady Harewood, and the staff who had alighted the car had to jump out of the way! I have also met pop stars and politicians and many famous people and I have enjoyed every minute of it.

I moved to Knaith in the late 1990s and it has a very special place in my heart. It may be small but it is steeped in history. The church of St Mary's I am very fond of as it is a church like no other.

Knaith has been a settlement for many hundreds of years, clinging on to that tiny, tiny hill. We lived in Terrace House Farm which got its name from the lord of the manor who lived in Knaith Hall. He wanted to reconfigure his garden in the 15/16th century so the road separating us from the church couldn't have been there then. He got rid of the village and relocated it to where Terrace House Farm is now, our house was on the top terrace of the garden giving it the name Terrace House Farm.

There are two main roads through the village. One is the drive to the farm and the other you can still see if you look at the white cottage at the bottom of the field. There is an avenue of trees that marks where the road used to be. The village itself used to be in the fields I owned in between those two houses, I have used metal detectors in there and there were definitely signs of habitation, as well a civil war musket ball. That area featured in the bruising encounter resulting in the Duke of Devonshire being killed, and the rout by the Roundheads that resulted in them being driven over Lea marshes, there is a memorial on Foxby Hill to commemorate that battle.

My hobbies are social history and the English and American civil war and I love to read about how people tick...what causes make you feel so passionate about them that you would go against your family and neighbours in war. I spend a lot of money on books regarding social history and civil wars.

I always wanted to live in Lincolnshire. My wife comes from Yorkshire and although we were living in Leeds we went to look at a house somewhere near Marton which it turned out wasn't for us, but on the way back we were driving to Gainsborough when we spotted the house in Knaith. I had done a bit of reporting out that way as well about the Marton Feast, a very ancient and hallowed festival, and knew that there were some lovely friendly people there and it was a lovely part of the world that I always want to live in. I have nothing against cities but I am a country man at heart and loved the thought of living near a river. I loved being by the Trent and would enjoy it when the Aegir arrived (a tidal bore), although it is not as big now since they dug up the causeway between Marton and Littleborough.

After moving into Terrace House Farm we spent a lot of blood, sweat and tears improving it and turned it into a lovely family home with lots of original features. I remember we celebrated the millennium in our garden in Knaith letting off fireworks, then I said to one of my daughters, Emma, "We won't see the new century start until we see the sunrise over the brass strip of the Meridian Line in Cleethorpes".

I have three daughters, Georgina works for Bobby Brown as a makeup artist in Sheffield, Emma is a corporate tax lawyer in London and Claire, who is a working mum, who works in Lincoln in accounts. I also have a lovely wife called Julie so I have four women in my life to keep me in order and I love them all to bits.

I left Yorkshire Television after 30 years for pastures new as the job was getting to be a young man's game. I was used to going out on outside broadcasts and travelling the world with a crew but because of cutbacks, something I am very aware of in the public sector, and the way that news is produced, there are now single crews so the reporter will go out with the cameraman and the sound crew and do everything themselves. I could never have done that and it grated with me so I left and became a freelance journalist and voiceover artist for various videos and CDs, and for private individuals covering all manner of subjects. My favourite was working for a company called Video 125 producing specialist videos about all aspects of trains.

While I was doing that I actually got a job a couple of days a week helping the police authority in Lincolnshire with the press and general PR, so I spent years doing that. I got to know how the police force works in Lincolnshire and the officers who pound the beat, and also the movers and shakers, and I admired them greatly. When the time came to elect a police and crime commissioner I thought that despite not being a political person and with the belief that politics and policing shouldn't mix, I put a tender in and was elected.

I was elected as the police and crime commissioner for Lincolnshire in 2012. The one thing in common with my previous job was that it was all about people and what I could do for them. They brought me their problems and occasional bouquets, as well as brick bats, and I did my best as their first police and crime commissioner for Lincolnshire to keep them safe. Along with the chief constable I was responsible by law for the safety and security of over 750000 people. It is not something that is delegated to a committee, I was it and if anything went wrong it was my fault. It was a very tough but very rewarding job.

We moved in 2007 to Grayingham where we are living today. I have had a very rewarding, varied and exciting life for which I am very thankful.

Alan Hardwick

KNAITH IN PICTURES

Knaith Hall with St Mary's to the left

Plans showing the modifications to St Mary's church

An early picture of a fancy dress party being held at Knaith Hall, date unknown

An early sketch of Knaith Hall

Laughterton Post Windmill. Full story on page 81

LAUGHTERTON

According to the village description drawn up for the millennium, Laughterton was called Leugttrican in about 680, which was possibly a variant spelling of Leagttricoun. (Spelling was not standardised at this time so it is common to have variant spellings.) The old English name was Leahtri dun, meaning hill or homestead where lettuce grew!

VILLAGE TALES

Crash Means 'Smash' in Laughterton

Residents of Laughterton may recall in 1996/7 the lorry that crashed into the wall of a house, shedding its full load of potatoes.

Lynn Peters, then member of the parish council, recalls the aftermath of the accident: "It was chaos, with potatoes strewn everywhere and the road blocked for hours, although luckily no-one was hurt and the driver walked away with only minor injuries."

Coincidentally, the lorry firm name was Burnett, which was also the name of the homeowners.

I suppose it was mashed potatoes all round for the residents of Laughterton that week!

Kettlethorpe School

Laughterton once had its own school which was situated on land that is now occupied by two residential properties, called Bell Lodge and Studio Cottage, the latter once the schoolmaster's home. It was a public elementary school called Kettlethorpe rather than Laughterton School, since it was named after the Kettlethorpe estate on which it stood.

The school was opened in 1854. By 1903 it was known as Kettlethorpe CE School and by the early 1950s the school was closed, thus having lasted for about 100 years. The period photo shows pupils and head teacher of the school, Mr Stevenson, in 1909. Mr Stevenson was previously head teacher just down the road at Newton on Trent school and transferred from there to Kettlethorpe School in 1906.

Kettlethorpe School, 1909. The man in the mortar board was Mr William Stevenson, headmaster of the school for 16 years and for many years also the organist at Kettlethorpe church.

Curiously, chalked on the board is 'Laughterton School' rather than Kettlethorpe School. This was evidently the favoured spot for school photos since the scene looks the same as in the 1909 photo. They could have even used the same bench!

Laughterton Past & Present

Laughterton's main street in the early 1930s. Blossom farmhouse is on the right with the chimney stack of today's village post office and shop (currently closed) visible in the background.

What does the snapshot of Laughterton's main street tell us about visible change over the past 70 years or so? Firstly, there has been significant growth in street furniture: telegraph lines, street lighting and so on, but notice the house and picket fence on the right, it seems little has changed there, though the small building behind has vanished and the post office has been covered in white paint. The roofline of the houses on the left looks the same, with no new introductions. So overall, the main street hasn't changed that much. I wonder what will happen over the next 70 years.

Laughterton Post Windmill

For 170 years the picturesque white-painted windmill at Laughterton was a benign sentinel over the village and in its working days provided valuable sustenance to both man and beast. Known as a post mill because the white body carrying the milling machinery and sails was mounted above a huge oak post which enabled the sails to be turned into the wind manually by a long tailpole at the rear. The basic design was evolved in the 12th century and primitive post mills were recorded in Lincolnshire by the 1170s.

A carving of a millstone and inscription recording miller John Bartle in 1781 was to be found on the inside of one of the upper entrance doors. The mill originally stood at Mill Hill, near Sandfield Farm (NGR: SK 8306 7630), but was moved to its final position on an artificial mound in Marsh Lane prior to 1828. Numerous post mills were moved to different sites either because the lease on the land expired or to find a better windblown site.

The four sails were mounted to a cast iron canister at the nose of the wooden axle, known as a windshaft. Each sail had a set of canvas-covered shutters which could be opened and closed in unison like a Venetian blind. A coiled spring mounted on each sail held these shutters

closed against the strength of the wind, adjustments to the spring tension could be made from the ground with each sail at rest in its lowest position to give variable driving power. The rotating sails turned two large wooden wheels on the windshaft, the front one was called a brake wheel because a wooden brake band could be brought into contact with the outer circumference of this wheel to stop the sails. A ring of wooden cogs on this and the tail wheel enabled the upper or runner stone to be rotated above a fixed bedstone to grind the grain. At some point in the 19th century the wooden teeth were replaced by a ring gear of finer pitched cast iron teeth.

The front pair of stones on the upper floor were made from a hard 'French burr' which was renowned for producing fine wheatmeal to make flour after sieving. The rear pair of millstones were of millstone grit from the Pennines, usually referred to as Peak or grey stones, these were used mainly for grinding animal feeds. A two-storied porch extension to the rear of the mill body, called the buck, housed grain-cleaning and flour-dressing machines. A spacious roundhouse enclosed the subframe or trestle supporting the main post and served as a granary or store.

The mill operated by wind until the late 1930s, the last pair of new sails were made in 1925 by a millwright from Metheringham called Lawson. By 1930 the Peak stones had been removed to a nearby outbuilding and were engine-driven on a wooden table or hurst frame. The power mill continued in operation until the early 1950s.

The old veteran, outdated by new technology and cheaper mass-produced products from the large roller mills of Gainsborough and elsewhere, was made redundant. She gradually succumbed to old age and the ravages of the weather. In 1951, by then in a derelict state, the mill was demolished by George Hewitt from Heapham Mill. The windshaft with its gear wheels and the upper part of the post were displayed outside the Mill House at Heapham for many years.

Before the advent of engine power the miller was totally reliant on the vagaries of the wind. Mr Mitchell, the last miller, told an amusing tale whose sentiment would have been shared by many an old-time miller. He complained that the wind often blew

Laughterton Mill

best on Sundays when he wasn't allowed to grind, "I am going to stop up until midnight to put the mill to work on the first minute of Monday. But there the wind is sure to drop! I put my head out of my bedroom window at midnight and sure enough the wind had dropped!"

A visit to the restored post mill at Wrawby near Brigg on an open day will enable the visitor to experience what it must have been like to operate Laughterton mill which was of similar design.

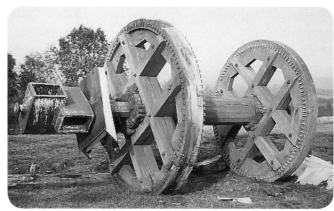

School Days in Laughterton

In 1996 the late Geoff Lidgett of Poplar Farm, Fenton, was asked to recall his memories of school life. The letter was recently rediscovered by his wife, Sarah, who has kindly let us print his memories. Geoff went to the school that used to be based in Laughterton but no longer exists and his memories highlight a school life very different from that of today.

Poplar Farm
Fenton
14/5/1996

Dear Thomas

Hopefully the following is the information you require.

I started school in 1924 at Laughterton, the next village a little over one mile away, 8.00am-4.00pm five days a week, walking a little over one mile wet or fine, several years later a few had cycles, please remember this was during a real depression. Two classrooms, junior and senior each heated by a coke stove which glowed red hot on top on cold days, *lighting provided by two paraffin lamps in each.*

No uniform, lunch taken in a satchel with a bottle of possibly cold tea, later some (few) had flasks for a hot drink, water was provided from a tank in one of the schoolhouse outbuildings, a tank was filled by pumping from a well by some of the senior pupils, a pipe protruded through the wall with a tap, attached to that was an enamelled mug with a chain shared by all.

The toilets were earth closets, no running water for flushing, two hand bowls for washing, one for girls and juniors, other for older boys, each on a stand with water which appeared to be thick soup at the end of the day. Lunch was eaten in the playground if fine, on wet days all crowded into the cloakroom, packed like sardines in a tin, you were not allowed in school to eat.

Two playgrounds, juniors and girls in one, boys in the other, and the surface was clinker near the building and soil the remainder, which was waterlogged in wet weather providing us with entertainment digging grips hopefully draining the water away.

Slates and slate pencils in the junior section followed by exercise books later, pencils and rubbers provided.

Geoff Lidgett

 A picture of Laughterton school pupils in 1940

The History of Jim Page Campsite

The parish of Kettlethorpe, in whose parish the campsite was, stands in the isolated corner of Lincolnshire at the southwest tip of Lindsey. It is bounded by the River Trent to the west, Nottinghamshire to the south and the angled Fossdyke to the east and north, a parcel of some three thousand acres including, besides the manor village, two hamlets, Fenton and Laughterton.

It had formed part of the Saxon Wapentake or Hundred or Well, and owed feudal dues to the Bishop of Lincoln under whom the memorial right was held. It had never been a prosperous or especially productive manor, then suited only to the growth of hay, flax, hemp and suchlike and most of the land being virgin forest for the pleasure of its lords. Earlier owners such as the de la Croix had held large holdings elsewhere to supplement rents.

Charles Hall was a Member of Parliament, as was his grandson, another Charles Hall, who died in 1743 and was succeeded by his step-nephew, Charles Amcotts of Harrington, High Sheriff of Lincolnshire in 1753 and Member of Parliament for Boston from 1768. His coat of arms is carved in stone and can be seen above the entrance door of the present hall.

On the death of Charles Amcotts, who was unmarried in 1777, Kettlethorpe passed to his sister who was the wife of Wharton Emerson MP, who forthwith took his wife's surname of Amcotts and was later made a baronet. He and his wife had one child, Elizabeth, who was married in 1780 to Sir John Ingilby of Ripley, Yorkshire.

Elizabeth, Lady Ingilby-Amcotts, died in 1812 and Kettlethorpe Hall became much dilapidated during the ownership of her son, Sir William Amcotts-Ingilby, a somewhat eccentric person who represented Lincolnshire in parliament from 1823 to 1834 and died without issue in 1854. Colonel Weston Cracroft-Amcotts (MP, 1866-74) who registered the estate under the Land Transfer Act in 1869 had inherited the estate in 1857 on the death of his mother who was the sister of Sir William Amcotts-Ingilby, the previous owner. Upon the death of Colonel Western-Craycroft Kettlethorpe passed to his youngest son, Major Frederick Cracroft-Amcotts in 1883 and upon his death in 1897 to his widow Emily Grace Cracroft-Amcotts.

Lady Emily Grace lived at Kettlethorpe Hall until her death on the 13th October 1936. She was greatly interested in the Scout Movement and the Rover Scouts from Gainsborough were granted to use part of the estate for camping where they constructed a log cabin in the woods. After the death of Lady Emily the woods and shooting rights were let to a syndicate from Sheffield and the scouts suffered the loss of their camping rights.

As successor to his mother Lady Emily, Sir Weston Cracroft Amcotts of Hackthorn gave the use of other land off Marsh Lane at Laughterton for other scouting activities. This was two plots containing 1.474 acres of woodland and 8.616 acres of pastureland. When the estate came into the hands of George Coldham Knight in early 1942 the whole estate was offered for sale (save the hall and grounds, which were retained by Sir Western), which meant the scouts would face the loss of their camping ground for a second time.

The then District Commissioner, Mr James (Jim) Page of Willingham by Stow wrote to George Coldham Knight's solicitors enquiring what figure the two plots of land on Marsh Lane, Laughterton, that they had used for camping since 1936, would likely fetch in the auction. The purchase price quoted was well out of reach of the local Scout Association but several days later Jim received a personal letter from George C Knight saying that he wished to give the land to him for the use of the local scouts. The one condition was that if scouting in Gainsborough ever fell through the land was to go for the use of the children of Laughterton and Kettlethorpe.

From April 19th 1942 until October 19th 1964 the site went by the name of District Campsite at Laughterton.

In 1964 the Gainsborough and District Boy Scouts Association, when Jim Page had the grand title of honorary District Commissioner, decided to acknowledge, "with sincere appreciation the valuable contribution to Scouting in the district made by Mr J Page, who had given untiring effort and devoted service to the movement throughout his life".

As of 19th October 1964, the campsite became known as The Jim Page Campsite. A commemorative certificate was presented to Jim Page which was signed by H Clarke (the Chairman) and Sidney A Davison (the Secretary) of the Gainsborough District Boy Scouts Association.

In later years Jim Page continued his scouting in the Gainsborough district as honorary District Commissioner, still supporting the work that was being done in scouting and enjoying regular trips to his campsite.

In early 1950 a metal-framed cabin was erected on the site and a water supply taken from the local farm. The water tap was placed adjacent to the main gate where many trips across the site must have been made to gain for water for camping.

Not a lot is known about the early history of the site but in 1968 the metal-framed building was demolished and thanks to help by Calvert, who assisted financially to pay for a new wood-framed cabin, it still stands on the site today.

The cabin was formally opened in 1969 and named the Calvert Cabin. Due to changes in lifestyle where earth toilets were dug and backfilled for each camp, permanent toilets were installed (complete with an underground waste tank) on the site in early 1970. The water supply was extended from the front gate to still a single tap on the back of the toilet block.

Gas water heating was also installed in the toilets to help with personal washing. This toilet block was extended in 1987 to the building that now stands on the site.

In the late 1960s a wooden kitchen was built at the end of the Calvert Cabin and this was used with great success until the new brick-built kitchen was constructed in the early 1990s. The Calvert Cabin and toilet block were originally lit by gas lights and eventually this was changed to electric lighting, first by a generator and then in the mid-1980s by its own electrical supply.

One of the great blows to the site was the loss of the elm trees on the eastern end of the site. The original site as detailed above had an area of 1.474 acres of woodland, this woodland consisted of a great many mature elm trees that made up a barrier of trees at the river end of the site. This was called the 'Spinney' and although the trees were tightly spaced camping was not possible, but for backwoods and other scout crafts this was just the place needed to complete the site.

In the mid-1970s Dutch elm disease struck and this hit the site badly. The trees on the site, plus many others that ran in a straight line across many other fields owned by other landowners, were killed, leaving great areas in the local area with just stumps of very hard and unusable wood. This took many years to clear but when complete it did provide additional areas to camp on and gave an area that we now call the 'Visitors Site'.

Next to come was a new shower/ladies toilet block that allowed the site to be used by greater numbers and provided showering facilities when required. Changes over the years have seen the water supply taken around the campsite, all to make the camping experience more acceptable to the modern way of living.

Power has been taken around the site, first to a kiosk next to the notice board and of late to the pole store and camp fire circle end of the site. This has allowed groups to have a power supply for lights and power for fridges that all make it easier to camp.

MY STORY

Don Weaver

I moved to Laughterton village in 1934 aged nine. The village was a lot different in those days with only 30 dwellings, a village school, the public house and a shop, all situated on the main road. There were no houses on Newton road and a lot of the village was owned by the Amcotts family who lived in nearby Kettlethorpe Hall. Services in the village were also very limited with no running water, electricity or proper sewerage. In those days you only had a pump for water and all the lights used to be oil lamps. Electricity didn't come to the village until 1937 and seemed amazing that you could flip a switch to get light! Mains water eventually arrived in 1940 and Don's house was the only house to have a tap!

I attended the local school based in Laughterton between the ages of 9 and 14 and remember that although the school was based in Laughterton at that time, Fenton used to be the village with the most number of children and they all made the walk from

Fenton to Laughterton daily. The school buildings themselves were owned by the Amcotts family but the school was run by the then Lindsey County Council.

School life was very different to today with the morning mainly being taken up by lessons in religious script. Mrs Amcotts was a regular visitor to the school and was very strict on discipline, woe betide you if you did not open the door as she approached, and if you saw her passing in the car on the street you had to stand at the side of the road and salute, and it soon got back to the school if you didn't, where the cane would await you! The school was eventually closed in the late 1940s where children were moved to either Newton or Torksey school.

My father did not work on the local farms as many of the residents did. Instead, he ran a joinery shop in the village where he would earn 18-30 shillings a week which would cover their rent and pay for a large garden to grow vegetables for the family. Most households also kept their own pig for meat and the shop and pub in the village also kept cattle and in particular, cows for milk to sell at the door. I recall that being able to get a house in Laughterton was not just a case of having enough money for rent. You had to go to Kettlethorpe Hall to discuss religion and be interviewed and your skills assessed before you were given a property.

I remember my early life in Laughterton with fond memories. It was a very much a community place which was administered through Kettlethorpe Hall, and people regularly enjoyed attending the whist drives and dances, and up to the start of the 2nd World War there were a lot of lads about. When I left school, I became an apprentice wheelwright and joiner and as a result was exempt for signing up for the war as wheelwrights and joiners were needed to keep industry going during those dark times. In 1935 I remember with fondness the Silver Jubilee of King George the V. This was a massive day with a big sports parade and a marvellous tea at Kettlethorpe Hall with large cuts of meat cut at the table supplied by Addison's from Fenton.

Money was very precious in my early years. Len Baker from Fenton once came over on his bike to ask if I wanted to go to the pictures in Lincoln to watch a submarine film and we sat in the 6p seats, I remember that on returning from Lincoln my mum reprimanded me because I wasn't really allowed to go and also for spending so much money!

One Friday I was on my bike when four buses pulled up all arriving from Leeds. These were evacuees but why were they arriving on this particular Friday? Because war was due to start the following Sunday and they were to be rehomed between Newton, Fenton and Torksey. This doubled the size of the school and more teachers were drafted in to deal with the large number of pupils.

This influx of people soon started to change Laughterton, it was all very sleepy at first but with more people moving to the village a lot of football started to be played and Laughterton formed its own team which soon began to win games against Torksey and Newton. The Territorial Army also used to come across from Mansfield for weekend camps and we would often play a game of football with them.

During the war I also took responsibility for firewatch, there were special constables in those days who organised this important role and a year later I also became part of the home guard. In times of war you had to belong to something to support the war effort and would often get inspected by the manpower board to ensure that your subscription for national service could still be deferred.

After the war and during the 1950s I remember how Laughterton began to change. Up to about the 1950s there had been no privately-owned land as it was part of the Kettlethorpe estate. But once the estate was sold off in parcels of land, interest grew in private housing and firms were invited to tender to build council houses. There was so much demand for housing that Italian labourers were brought in to cope with the demand and the first building machinery was introduced which did the work of ten men. They soon were building 1000 homes a day nationally.

In 1957 I married the love of my life, Winnie, in Kettlethorpe church with a wedding reception in the village hall. We set up home together in Laughterton where we have lived ever since.

Over the years I have seen a lot of change in Laughterton and I have noticed how people moved from the towns to live a quieter rural life, at first it seemed strange to a lot of people to leave the hustle and bustle of a city but they liked the environment. The village has grown and expanded over the years but I still like living here with Winnie and the memories of village life throughout good and difficult times are still happy memories for me.

LAUGHTERTON IN PICTURES

Home Farm Laughterton pre-build

Home Farm in the winter 2000

Home Farm Laughterton after build

Home Farm Laughterton part way through the build

Jim Porter in his van. Full story on page 99

MARTON & STOW PARK

Marton – the name is derived from the Saxon for farm (or hamlet) on the marsh – is a small village on the A156, lying about five miles south of Gainsborough, with a population of between 400 and 500 people.

Introduction

As a vivid reminder of the days when sailing boats made their trade along the river - the river used to be busy with tugs towing strings of barges to Lincoln or Boston - there is a blue anchor dredged from the Trent and now displayed in front of the village church. The coming of the railways in the mid-19th century led to a severe decline in river trade and the river was allowed to become silted up and partially blocked by wrecks, possibly the anchor came from one of these.

VILLAGE TALES

The Old Village School

The village school, with its chequered brickwork and small bell tower, was built in 1846 for a maximum of 63 children. It stood for 116 years until it was replaced in 1962 by the current Marton Primary School in Stow Park Road. The old school's site was then occupied by St Margaret's home for the elderly.

The old village school, with charming chequered brickwork and small bell tower.

Marton Chapel

The Wesleyan chapel built in 1814

Marton Chapel, built in 1814, is thought to be the second oldest chapel in Lincolnshire still in use. Services are held every Sunday from November to March at 3pm and from April to October at 6pm. There is a coffee morning on the last Wednesday of the month at 10am. Currently there is a congregation of 20.

The chapel has always been actively involved in

the village. In the 1950s–70s there was a large Sunday school but this has sadly had to close although the annual Skegness outing continues.

 Photo of Marton Sunday School, taken sometime in the 1950s, with Mrs Constance Kitchinson (left) and Mrs Henrietta Holman (right).

The annual Skegness outing and Mr Harry Williams, who drove the bus for many years, is being presented with a tankard by Mrs Doris Kitchinson. Also pictured are children from the Sunday school and Mrs Sheila Worrell (left) and Mrs Gwen Molson (right).

Littleborough Ferry

The remains of a Roman causeway can be seen at extreme low tides in the River Trent. There was a ferry here for centuries, carrying goods and people across the Trent River to Littleborough.

Littleborough ferry existed due to the military road that was built by the Romans. This road left the main road at Doncaster cutting through Bawtry, Everton, Clayworth, Wheatley and Sturton-Le-Steeple,

and eventually joined Ermine Street at Scampton, Lincolnshire. The road was taken across the Trent by means of a massive stone causeway 18 feet wide and 12 feet high, that was built in the time of Emperor Harden (117-138 AD). On the eastern bank the road continued in a straight line through Marton and Sturton-by-Stow, the road is now called Stow Park Road and, beyond the railway crossing, Till Bridge Lane.

The causeway could only be used at low tide, at other times the river crossing had to be made by a chain ferry which continued in use until the 1900s. This was one of the oldest ferries in England and the remnants of the machinery can still be seen near the ramp into the river.

A small rowing boat ferrying passengers across the River Trent at Littleborough.

Marton Mill

The tower of this small mill has been conserved by a sympathetic owner in recent years. It enjoys a commanding view of the River Trent, standing on a bluff above the east bank of this ancient port, west of Marton village. Advertised for sale by auction in 1799 by the owner, John Clarke, a noted millwright from Morton near Gainsborough; this may signify its recent construction. Clarke built on spec a number of post mills and the small tower at Marton, well blown on the high bank of the Trent, would be of similar capacity to a post mill. However, a tower provided a sturdier and roomier building and the transition from the direct drive of a post mill to the newer spur gear layout gave a higher ratio of sail to millstone revolutions. By 1853 it had gained two spring sails to replace earlier commons. In its later working life it had four patent sails and drove a pair of French, and a pair of grey stones with a flour dresser.

Both Marton and Gate Burton post mill were owned jointly by a succession of Marton men, including Charles Morris in the 1820s, followed by

Marton Mill, 1927

W Stevens c.1832 & 1840, and a John Bottomley until his bankruptcy in 1852. Following Bottomley's occupation the mill was operated as a subscription mill until at least 1863. Subscription or Union mills were owned by a group of local shareholders, often small farmers, to grind their grain by employing a tenant miller. This type of early stock company was popular before and after the Napoleonic War when grain and flour prices were at a premium. A number of other mills in Gainsborough and surrounding area were operated on this basis at one time including ones at Upton, Sturton by Stow, Epworth and Lincoln.

The photograph above shows the mill complete in 1927, it had been stripped to an empty shell by Easter 1928.

Marton, Trent Port 1926

The Old Mill in recent years

St Margaret of Antioch Church

At the centre of the village is the Anglican parish church of *St Margaret of Antioch*. The building is a mixture of Anglo-Saxon and Norman styles and has an 11th century tower of traditional Saxon herringbone stonework.

In the west wall of the porch are the remains of what is thought to be a Saxon cross shaft, laid horizontally in the masonry. In the chancel is a small crucifix that was discovered during building work on the church. The crucifix is unusual in that Jesus' feet are separated, rather than overlapped, as is common.

In the churchyard there is a tall cross, probably a medieval market or butter cross - a type of medieval English market cross associated with English market towns - that commemorates villagers who gave their lives serving in the world wars.

During alterations in 1868 a carved stone crucifix was found. Unusually, Christ's feet are shown separated. Its age is uncertain, though probably 12th century.

Left and above, St Margaret's Parish Church

The Black Swan Guesthouse

The Black Swan as seen from High Street, Marton

The Black Swan guesthouse stands at the junction of the A156 and Stow Park Road, (leading into Till Bridge Lane) part of a Roman road that runs from Ermine Street (the A15) to Doncaster, via the River Trent ford at Littleborough.

A grade 2 listed building, the Black Swan was built on the site of a previous property called *The Black Swan Posting House*. Part of the cellar of this original building still remains.

The classical Georgian style building you see today was constructed in three stages. The oldest part is the main house seen from the road which dates back to about 1760. What were originally barns were built next and then a two-storey linking building was built between the house and barn in the early 19th century. The barn, with the arched entrance to the enclosed yard and stables, was at one time a ropery, a place where ropes were made. There is still a hit-and-

The courtyard with the main house in the background. The stables and interior arrangements of the house remain much as they have always been

miss window in the private dining room of the main house which would once have opened out into the archway, allowing the occupants to see how many people were arriving by horse-drawn coach.

Marton was an important halt for drovers en route to Newark from Gainsborough and some of the droves were upwards of a mile in length. Cattle and sheep owners usually stayed at the Black Swan and the White Swan, providing work through the night for numerous local blacksmiths. As an inn, the Black Swan was permitted to remain open as long as a bed was empty, offering basic accommodation, simple victuals, home-brewed ale, and stabling to the lawful traveller.

Inside the dining room there are some shards of glass, now in a frame, that were part of the original window, bearing a scratched inscription.

The fragment of glass in the photograph at top left has the word 'Dear' and below that 'Sweet', the fragment top right has 'of Ga', and the bottom fragment shows 'May 17', all written in a charming cursive script. The full original text was: 'Dear Betsy Whitmoure of Gainsburgh May 17 – 1779 Sweet heavenly maid'

Like other inns and alehouses in rural Lincolnshire, the Black Swan brewed its own ale; the popular parish drink was a form of malty mild; heavy, dark, sweet and strong, that varied considerably from brew to brew. The average county gravity was 1060, the second highest in England. Georgian and Victorian licensing hours were long, 18 hours a day, 4am to 10pm, seven days a week, closed only during Divine Service, Christmas Day and Good Friday.

Farmer John Abraham was the last innkeeper of the Black Swan. He was recorded in the 1841 census

aged 45, with his wife Ann aged 45 and family of four: Elizabeth 15, Ann 15, John 15, and Mary 5. They had two guests and employed two servants.

It is believed that the Black Swan was a coaching inn until 1860. Certainly, by the time of the 1871 census the property was recorded as *Manor Farm*, by which time it had ceased trading as a coaching inn following development of the railway, particularly as there was now a station up the road towards Sturton.

Manor Farm remained the name until 1993 when the property was bought by Brian and Myra Cunliffe, who fully renovated it, opening it once again as *The Black Swan Coaching Inn Guest House*. Since buying the property they have now added a further two letting rooms to the eight which were originally here.

During removal of the fireplace various papers and visiting cards were discovered, having dropped down behind the mantelpiece. One of them had been there for 133 years.

One thing you really don't need is to have an articulated lorry coming at speed through your dining room window (this occurred in 1980).

Here is the front end of the lorry clad with the shattered remains of the window and supporting brickwork. (The bend in the road has since been smoothed to ensure safer driving in this area.)

The Circle of Life

It's hard to believe in today's politically correct health conscious society, that an adult could possibly say to an eleven-year-old boy, *"The best thing you could do lad, is have a pint of ale and a pipeful of tobacco"*. Rightly or wrongly, this was the advice given by my great-grandfather Herbert Wright to my father Horace Spencer in 1906! There was however a sound reason for this advice and I'm quite sure the old man had his grandson's best interests at heart.

In 1895 Herbert Wright was the landlord of the Railway Inn at Stow Park on the B1500 between Sturton-by-Stow and Gainsborough, now a private house. He was also a dealer in 'fallen', or dead animals known as the cadman, or knackerman. Most villages had one, as the density of farm animals was much greater then than today. With no mechanical transport all movements of carcasses were by horse and cart. As one might imagine, loading a dead horse or cow weighing half a ton or more onto a cart three to four feet off the ground presented somewhat of a problem. Knackermen were an enterprising breed, and soon devised specially adapted two wheeled 'knackers' carts' to ease the operation.

Once in the yard, the carcass was carefully dismembered, the skin going to a tannery, the better bones were sent to a cutlery factory for handles and the remainder was boiled to make tallow, glue or fertiliser, nothing was wasted. Local footballers were known to visit the yard to soak their boots in the oil to keep them supple, and to buy horse liniment to rub on their aching joints. Many country landlords were similarly obliged to supplement their income, plying various trades in an attempt to provide a reasonable living for their families, it must be remembered that pubs at the time only sold drink, although some did take in lodgers. The clientele of the Railway

Inn consisted of local farm workers, passing horse traffic and a number of railway workers from the nearby station and goods yard. Like many country pubs the Railway had several acres of land on which great-grandfather kept pigs, chickens, a cow and of course horses, being the main form of transport at the time. In some respects it was yesteryear's version of 'The Good Life', a largely self-sufficient enterprise which provided most of the food for the family, the difference being, this was not for amusement, but out of sheer necessity.

Great-grandfather was well known for his eccentricities and like most old men he despised change. In later years when traffic lights were first introduced into Gainsborough, he would tell 'Taffy' his pony, to *"Git on,"* and drive his trap straight through on red saying, *"I've bin cummin' ere long before they iver thought a bloody traffic lights"*.

Born at Welbourn in 1855 to a family of wheelwrights, he was known in our family as 'pretty face', not for his good looks, but for his habit of telling the grandchildren they had pretty faces. He took over the Railway Inn in 1895, the same year my father was born. An article in the Chronicle and Leader reporting his and my great-grandmother's diamond wedding celebrations during his eightieth year, with an accompanying photograph taken in the bar of the Railway Inn, reports him as saying *"I want you to take my photograph playing dominoes with these other old boys"*. He goes on to say how he had happy memories of the 'good old days', and how he would stop off school to help his mother brew beer, *"The beer in those days was the proper stuff! Forty years ago beer was 3d a pint, now it's 6d, and nowhere near as good"*. His companion William Deeks of Marton is quoted as saying *"I used to walk to school with my friend. We used to smoke half an ounce of tobacco on the way, and had a quart of ale for lunch"*.

On father's eleventh birthday, 8th November 1906, great-grandfather decided it was high time he learned something of the finer art of the knacker trade, which it was thought at the time, father might eventually follow into. Father, who by all accounts was a quiet and sensitive lad, had little enthusiasm for the job, being more interested in music, two more dissimilar professions would be impossible to imagine, however, great-grandfather provided him with one of his leather aprons, tied around his waist with a length of binder band, and instructed him to *"Sit on the bench in the yard with ya back to the wind"*. *"You'd best start on something small,"* he said, dragging a dead sheep from the shed bloated to twice its

Mike's great-grandfather and Mrs Herbert Wright

Mike's father, Horace Spencer (centre) date, around 1930

normal size. Dropping it at Father's feet and placing a large pointed knife in his hand, he instructed him as to where he should make his primary incision. Unaware great-grandfather had retired to a safe distance, and wanting to complete the procedure as quickly as possible, father plunged the knife into the sheep. He was instantly engulfed in a cloud of foul-smelling, gas putrid liquid and more than his fair share of maggots, as the rotting carcass hissed and groaned like a huge deflating balloon; he dropped the knife, ran to the other side of the yard and was violently sick. Great-grandfather, quietly amused, wiped him down and explained, *"The fost un's always the wost son'.* Father, doing his best not to cry, maintained his distance from the foul-smelling carcass. Great-grandfather chuckling to himself, wandered off towards the house. He returned a few moments later smoking his second-best pipe and carrying a pint of bitter. *"Ere lad! Keep having a puff on this, it'll help kill the smell. And if you av' a swig of ale now and then, it won't taste quite so bad."* I never knew whether or not father managed to complete the task, but without doubt it must have had a profound and long-lasting effect on him.

Two years later, at the age of thirteen, he left home and joined the Royal Marines School of Music in Portsmouth as a band boy, stating his age to be fourteen - the minimum allowable entry age at the time. After serving for a year this deception was discovered and as a result he lost a year's pay. He served in the band aboard the battlecruiser HMS Lion throughout the First World War, and fought at the battle of Jutland, during which he was awarded five shillings (25p) for good shooting. The mystery of why anyone would receive such an award when the ships engaged in the battle were several miles apart, was solved when I was interviewed in the early 1990s by a military historian carrying out research

for a television programme on Jutland. I discovered it was not for shooting a rifle as I had assumed, but the aiming of the huge 13½ inch guns which battered the German fleet. Following his discharge from the Navy in 1919, father spent most of the 1920s in the orchestras on the transatlantic liners - in particular the Mauritania - and played in both silent movie cinemas and the music halls, becoming known as one of the finest percussionists in the north of England and an accomplished writer. On 5th March, 1936, eight years before I was born, great-grandfather died aged eighty-one. My parents, brother and sister returned to Stow Park, where father took over as landlord of the Railway Inn, the place of his birth.

HE CHRONICLE & LEADER, SATURDAY, 16 NOVEMBER, **1935**

THREE JOLLY OLD BOYS!

Every Day They Take Their Drop—Of Beer And At Dominoes.

STOW DIAMOND WEDDING.

Octogenarian Licensee And His Wife Quietly Celebrate.

Mr. Herbert Wright and his friends at their daily dominoes in the Railway Inn bar, Stow Park. Mrs. Wright is on the left next to Mr. John Hurst, and Mr. William Deeks is on the right.

AN octogenarian licensee and his wife, Mr. and Mrs. Herbert Wright, of the Railway Inn, Stow Park, near Sturton, celebrate their diamond wedding to-day. A "Chronicle and Leader" representative who called on the couple at their home this week found the cheery old couple carrying on all the usual work of the public-house.

"I want you to take my photograph playing dominoes with these other old boys," Mr. Wright, who is 80, told the photographer. "I say old boys," he went on, "because I once saw a photograph of two lads of 17 shaking hands and saying 'How are you, old man?' Under another picture of two men of 70 it said 'How are you, old boy?' We are still old boys."

Daily Dominoes.

His companions were Mr. William Deeks, of Marton, who is 83, and Mr. John Hurst, of Marton, who is 79. Staunch pals, the old boys play dominoes every day.

It is forty years since Mr. and Mrs.

Wright went to the Railway Inn. They went from Welbourn, where Mr. Wright was born. He was the son of the village carpenter, and his schoolboy friend was the son of the village tailor—the late Field-Marshal Sir Wm. Robertson.

When Beer Was Beer.

He has some happy memories of the old days when he used to stay at home from school to help his mother to brew beer. Then he learnt his father's business, and at 17 went to Spridlington, where he earned 8s. a week. A little later he went back to Welbourn, where he met his future wife.

"The beer they had in those days was proper stuff," he says. When he became a licensee he took a couple of barrels of "house-brewed" with him and there's never been anything like it in the house since.

"Forty years ago beer was 3d. a pint, and whiskey was 3d. a glass. Now the prices are 6d. and 9d., and "it's not nearly so good."

Both he and Mrs. Wright say that it is nothing special that has kept them on their job for so long. It is just a matter of keeping at it, they say.

Teetotalism is not so good, avers a veteran licensee, but a man can ple himself how much he smokes. For many years he used to smoke 12 cigarettes a year—they were given to him by a traveller who was a regular caller each morning. Then he took to a pipe until he lost it years ago. He has never bothered to a new one.

Starting Young.

Each day when Mr. Deeks and Hurst call at the "Railway" the three boys play dominoes while Mrs. Wright watches them.

Mr. Deeks was apprenticed to a blacksmith in Suffolk. He remembers when he went to school with his friend they used to smoke half an ounce of tobacco on the way. For lunch they had a quart of beer. In his retirement he forsaken neither his pipe nor his glass.

The Marton Feast

We were lucky enough to be loaned some scrapbooks that were put together by some forward-thinking ladies of the village that contain newspaper clippings and photos of events from times gone by.

One thing that stood out and featured at least once in all of the books was the Marton Feast, which also incorporated the villages of Gate Burton and Brampton. It was a really big affair that seemed to span a whole week climaxing at the weekend with two days packed with events!

We know that the feast was a popular event a long time ago, however we do not have an exact date. It ceased sometime just before the Second World War and was re-instated some forty years later in 1978. It is from this date that our photos continue.

So ignoring the pun please feast your eyes on these wonderful photos taken across the years at the Marton Feast.

 An early picture of the Marton Feast, date unknown.

Feast of Fun at Marton Weekend from a Newspaper Article in 1978

After an absence of 40 years the 'Marton Feast' was revived at the weekend and many people hope it will once again be an annual event.

Much hard work was put in by committee members and many helpers, who ensured that all sections of the community could be involved in what proved to be a very successful and enjoyable time for all.

The feasting opened with a buffet and dance on Friday in a large marquee on the parish field and a large crowd enjoyed dancing to the music of the Jack Smith Sound and the Tornadoes disco.

Disco 'gogo' dancers contributed two interlude spots and the feast trio of Tim Farquhar, Roy Staniforth and Ian Kitchinson sang.

A raffle for a large piece of beef was won by Mrs G Roach, and a hardworking group of ladies handled the mammoth task of providing refreshments for 300 dancers.

Saturday opened with the final of the Feast Cup junior football competition in which Sudbrooke beat Guinness 6-2.

Nail-driving...this time by Mr McNee - was a feature of Marton Feast.

The afternoon festivities began with a spectacular parade through the village led by the Lindsey Pipe Band, the East Stockwith Morris dancers, fancy dress competitors and the 1st Marton Scouts.

Chief guests were television newsman Alan Hardwick and his fiancé Miss Julie Cryer. Mr Hardwick performed the formal opening ceremony. Later joined by Councillor Mrs Jill Westgarth and Mr Nigel Taylor, Mr Hardwick and Miss Cryer judged the fancy dress competition.

Winners were: Infants - Phillip Molson and Ian Moles; Juniors - Emma Worrell and Tina Molson; Seniors – Mr B Gelder and Mr B Bealby.

Opener Alan Hardwick (former Calendar presenter & later Police Commissioner for Lincolnshire) receives instruction on the longbow from Mick Houghton at Marton Feast.

The judges received white carnation buttonholes and bouquets of carnations and chrysanthemums.

The Morris dancers gave a display, there was music from the pipe band, the Vikings high-wire act, an archery display by Mick Houghton and a tug-of-war competition which was won by Trentport with Bassetlaw as runners-up.

There were also various games and stalls and refreshments served by the helpers. A licensed bar was provided by the staff of the Castle Inn on Friday and Saturday evenings.

Winners of the various events were: Skittles, Mr Valley; clay pigeon shoot, Mr L Jubb; bean bags, Mrs Roe; miniature skittles, Miss Stear; tunnel ball, Miss Cryer; ski ball, Andrew Hill; target bean bags, Mrs Boylan; bowls, Clive Liversidge.

Children's sports were organised by Mrs Boylan and the winners each received certificates and prizes.

In the evening a disco was run for children in the marquee. Music was provided by Mrs Brignull and Robert Leaning. A whist drive took place in the parish hall with Mr W Gibson as MC. Winners were: ladies - Mrs Hewerdine, Mrs Moody and Ms Toulson; gents - Mr G Hill, Mr J Dixon and Miss Brown. Raffle winner was Mrs Hobbins; miniature drive winners Mrs Vickerman and Mr Robinson.

Winner of a Sunday fishing match was Keith Ford with a weight of 12½oz. Equal second were Mr D ford and Mr C Liversidge. In the afternoon a football match entertained a good crowd with the over 25s taking on the under 25s. The younger team won 5-4. A mock cup made by Mr Gelder was presented to the winning team and a bottle of champagne was opened. To close the Feast on Sunday evening a United Service was held in St Margaret's church, with a full attendance.

The service was taken by the Rev Cook of Saxilby and organist was Mrs Roach. The church was decorated by Mrs H Tudor. The collection was for the Feast funds.

The Whale That Came Up The Trent

From a newspaper article dated Sunday September 18th 1938

Several thousand people yesterday paid admission to see a two ton, 20' long whale which had been rammed by a petrol barge and caught in the River Trent near Gainsborough.

It is thought to be the mate of the whale which was caught at Keadby three weeks ago and which is now in the National History Museum in London. The second whale is believed to be a female, while that caught at Keadby was a male.

The whale caught at Gainsborough had been in the River Trent for three days. It remained in the neighbourhood of Keadby for two days but swam during the Friday night but at low tide. It was seen stranded on a sandbank at Marton five miles from Gainsborough and 70 miles from the sea - the farthest inland point at which a whale has been seen within living memory.

TERRIFIC STRUGGLE

On Saturday afternoon boatmen on a string of barges towed by the Tyne motor vessel of Hull, took two shots at the whale, but the shots ricocheted off its back into the water.

No efforts were made to catch it at Marton, but arrangements were being made by Superintendent I. Booth, of Gainsborough, to have it destroyed by humane methods when a report was received that it had been refloated by the tide.

The whale swam back to Gainsborough and was near the town when it was overtaken by the petrol barge Kestrel, with 90 tons of sand and gravel aboard, from Carlton, bound for Brigg, via the Ancholme.

The captain of the Kestrel Mr J Chapman of 18 Gordons Row, Newark, stated afterwards that he and his mate Mr Stanley Oglesby, of 10 Dewbury Terrace, Swann Street, Hull, had a terrific struggle with the whale for over an hour.

FOUGHT LIKE A TIGER

"It was 50 yards ahead" said Mr Chapman "and I ran my vessel at it, I was successful in hitting it, and turning round saw it fighting furiously in the water."

"I turned the vessel round and ran alongside and my mate, Oglesby, tried to get it with a boat hook. He was successful and we fastened it to the boat and brought it to Gainsborough."

Oglesby said that after the boat had been turned round and he'd stuck a boat hook into the whale, it

"Fought like a tiger".

"It threw water right over the boat and nearly drowned me," he said. "Chapman came to my aid and I lassoed its tail with a rope and pulled it tight, eventually getting it fast to the side, but it continued to fight vigorously, it was so strong that it prevented the boat being turned round again despite the fact that it was against the ebb and though our boat had a cargo of 90 tons of gravel."

"Eventually we got the boat round, the whale fought hard for some time but finally it drowned as we were towing it with its tail."

The whale was on view on behalf of the John Coupland Hospital, Gainsborough yesterday. It was taken from the river by a crane.

The total amount collected in admission fees yesterday in aid of the John Coupland Hospital was over £100, so that the whale was seen by about 12,000 people.

It is expected that it will be on view again tonight in aid of the nursing association.

No decision has been reached as to the future of the whale's carcass. The police are awaiting a decision by the Custom's Officer, who have been in consultation with the Receiver of Wrecks.

The Whale That Came Up The Trent.

MY STORY

Jim Porter

Marton has been fortunate to have had a number of community-minded people who help to make village life such a pleasure. One such person was Jim Porter. He was Marton's mobile grocer and the sight of his van, known as Big Bertha, became a familiar symbol of the care and attention that he lavished on his customers.

Jim with Big Bertha

Jim's dedication was publicly recognised in 1983 when he won £600 in prizes in a nationwide competition to find the ideal family trader. On Friday 7 October Jim and his wife Beryl were whisked off to London for a special reception at which he was chosen from thousands of nominations as one of the top six ideal traders in the British Isles. Jim was singled out because of his longstanding and unselfish devotion to others, over and above the call of duty.

As well as keeping the more vulnerable residents of the village well-supplied with groceries Jim would also deliver medical supplies for the elderly and raised money for local charities and voluntary organisations. After 50 years of dedicated service Jim finally sold his business to enjoy his gardening and walking but still remained an active part of community life.

Beryl Porter performing on the accordion

Concert for Silver Jubilee

In March 1977 a comedy concert was held in Marton Parish Hall in aid of the Royal Silver Jubilee celebration fund. Taking part were Mr & Mrs J Porter, Mr & Mrs I Kitchinson, Mr & Mrs C Leaning, Mr & Mrs P Fotheringham, Mrs Coote, Mr H Jubbs and Mr S Little. Comedy sketches, monologues, solo and community songs were performed and, along with a raffle, the total proceeds raised was £44.

Jim & Beryl Porter receiving Jim's award as one of Britain's top family traders from comedian Bob Monkhouse.

Concert party on stage for the opening number

Loraine Olsen

You know when you walk through Loraine's front gate that this is no ordinary house. The front garden is only a tantalising glimpse of the character it holds inside. The well-kept garden is full of all manner of interesting statues, lights & flowers, mixed in with a few dragons and gargoyles. We were greeted by Loraine who showed us into her beautifully eclectic home.

Loraine's house was highly polished with not an animal hair to be seen, and it was here in the lounge that we sat down, drank tea and let her tell her story which turned out to be a very interesting tale.

Loraine started dancing when she was three-years-old and it soon became evident that she had a real talent. Having attended one of the best dancing schools in Sheffield she won a scholarship to Sadler's Wells in London at the age of 15. To her bitter disappointment she was told that she was too tall to be a solo ballerina and a local newspaper ran her story, but luck was on her side and an agent for the famous Bluebell Girls read about her and invited her to audition. Her talent shone through and out of 250 hopefuls Loraine got one of the two vacancies being offered.

From the Paris nightclubs where Loraine started at 15, the Bluebell Girls went on a tour of Europe and their show in Rome was televised for Italian television weekly, however, because of the Italians' strict Catholic religion they were not allowed to

show their legs and had to wear thick black tights! It was while she was working for Italian television that she met The Merseybeats, Russ Conway and Matt Munro. The European tour lasted two years, after which Loraine had a yearning to visit America. Madame Bluebell didn't want her to go because she said she was too young and that once she went to America she wouldn't want to come back. Loraine set off, heading to Lake Tahoe in Nevada with Paul Steffan, a brilliant dancer and choreographer, where they did a show called Benvenuta Roma which was years ahead of its time with dance routines

similar to West Side Story. After a year, now aged 18, she returned to England and was quickly re-employed by Madame Bluebell for a forthcoming trip to Las Vegas.

Loraine aged 16 years

Loraine worked in the Stardust nightclub on the Las Vegas Strip and in 1968 she was crowned Miss Las Vegas. "I got to meet a lot of celebrities, James Garner, Liberace, Louis Armstrong and Frank Sinatra, and even meeting the Duke of Edinburgh on a beach in Greece! I presented Steve McQueen with a racing cup and made sure I got a kiss from him."

Loraine also recalls how she was lying on a blanket sunbathing at her apartment in Las Vegas when she got bitten by a scorpion. "I didn't realise at first but later on that night I collapsed on stage, the bite on my back left a big black mark which kept flaring up for years after the event."

When Loraine was 23 she met her husband Jorgen Olsen in Las Vegas, he was in show business as a flying trapeze artist, and they went to the Bahamas to work in exotic nightclubs and casinos. In the early 1970s they both came back to England to settle down, living at first in Derbyshire running a restaurant, and it was in here that Loraine and Jorgen had their son Yan. They then moved to Sheffield and opened an antique shop before briefly living in the rectory in the grounds of Gate Burton Hall. Loraine & Jorgen found a wonderful derelict house dating back to 1629 on the High Street in Marton village which with a lot of hard work was returned to its former glory. Loraine went on to have a daughter called Lisa, but still kept busy modelling for catalogues and magazines and working part time for a pharmaceutical company.

Loraine's children have long since flown the nest and her husband is no longer with her but Loraine doesn't rest, preferring to care for her animals. "I worked hard as a dancer," she said "and that ethos has never left me". As we leave we walk through the house and the dogs arrive jumping up to greet us, whilst a life-sized zombie waiter called Egbert bursts into life and offers us a drink...you couldn't make it up but you can see how this is a home with warmth, fun and eccentricities.

MARTON & STOW PARK IN PICTURES

A gathering at the war memorial

Marton High Street looking towads the Ingleby Arms on the left

The imminent demolition of the White Swan inn is announced in the local paper in 1959. This building stood opposite the Black Swan, which stands on the right corner, just out of view.

ANCIENT INN TO GO

Pupils of Marton School

Marton High Street - called Main Street when this photo was taken. The Ingleby Arms sign is visible at the end of the row of houses on the right, with the church just beyond. The village shop on the right later became Marton Post Office. Beyond the charmed group of children on the left is a garage.

Main Street, Marton, Nr. Gainsborough.

View over Marton taken some time in the 1950s

Marton High Street date unknown

Members of Marton junior football team

The riverside houses which used to be in close proximity to the Trent but now abandoned and in ruins due to persistent flooding some years ago.

High Street approached from the south, with the church on the left. On the right is the old Marton School, in front of which stands a camera-struck group of children.

The Ingleby Arms in 1950

The 1910 football team

The old fish & chip shop

Pupils of Marton School

Top row left to right: Mrs Rhodes, Jean Williams, Alan Spafford, Steve Spence, Sue Nicholson, Janet Burton, Jacqueline Moody, John Spafford, Chris Molson, Peter Moody, Dennis Williams, Shirley Clifton, Silvia Muir & Mrs Warwick

Second row left to right: Mike Spence, Pete Wyers, Rob Garner, Mary Charity, Bruce Magee, Malcolm Rook, Tony Nicholson, Trevor Tindale, Linda Cutts & Diane Locke

Third row left to right: Linda Clifton, David Williams, Linda Ford, Sue Spence, Linda Burton, Lorraine Robinson, Leslie Robinson, Trevor Moody, Eric Humphries, Pat Brignall & unknown

Fourth row left to right: Pauline Muir, Stuart Heppenstall, Dawn Spence, Maureen Ford, June Clifton, Christine Nicholson, unknown, Kevin Ford, David Scott & Lesley Humphries

Left is a garage sign painted on the building wall and beyond the garage is what looks like a shop or petrol pump paraphernalia.

Marton once had its own petrol station

Marton school pupils date unknown

Girl Guides parading in Marton

Mr & Mrs J Gibbs outside their fish & chip shop in Marton

Residents helping out during a firemans' strike

Marton Scout Group

105

Full photo & caption on page 113

NEWTON ON TRENT

The name Newton is derived from the old English niwe and tun, or 'new estate or village'. Newton lies 10 miles south of Gainsborough and 10 miles west of Lincoln. The River Trent lies to the west, crossed by Dunham Bridge. It has a population of some 300 plus residents, fluctuating from 399 in 1841 to as few as 194 in 1981.

VILLAGE TALES

A Brief History

In 1831-2 the Dunham toll bridge was built by a group of Lincolnshire businessmen for the princely sum of £18,854 - before this a ferry service linked Newton to Dunham. The proprietors bought the ferry, closed it, and charged a toll for crossing the bridge - that's private enterprise for you.

The bridge carries the A57 over the River Trent between Newton and Dunham on Trent, thus crossing from Lincolnshire into Nottinghamshire. It still stands on its original piers and abutments but its original cast iron superstructure was re-built in steel in 1976 to meet modern trunk road standards.

The bridge superstructure comprised four arches, resting on stone piers, each spanning 118 feet. The iron was cast at the Sheffield Park ironworks, contractors for the erection were Messrs Harmer &

The original Dunham Bridge, the structure now removed and only the supports remaining

Pratt, and a Mr George Leather was the chief engineer.

The toll for crossing the bridge ranged from one halfpenny per head of livestock to 1s/3d for a four-wheeled coach, chariot (!), chaise or hearse drawn by two horses. Steam engines had to pay an eye-watering shilling per wheel.

The original Dunham Bridge with its cast iron superstructure under demolition 1976

The floods in 2000 at Dunham Bridge

The corrugated iron-clad Kymes' Fish & Chip Shop in Trent Lane (c1950s), formerly the vicarage canteen. (Trent Lane is now Dunham Road.)

Members of the Kyme family outside Kelfield, 6 High Street, (c1910)

Newton on Trent went through a number of changes in the 20th century. In 1932 Newton saw its first fish and chip shop open, as the delightfully named Lil's Fish and Chip Shop. This was followed by Kymes' Fish & Chip Shop in 1935 which opened up behind the current post office. It relocated in 1951 to the site of the former vicarage corrugated iron canteen which had been re-erected in Trent Lane.

Edgar Kyme (left) and Frank Gelder. Two budding thespians in 'The Burst Pipe' sketch 1950.

The 2nd World War brought more changes. In 1940 a group of war evacuee schoolchildren and their teacher, Margery Coupe, arrived from Leeds. After the war, when the children returned to their homes, Margery stayed to marry Arthur Moore and to teach in the village school until her retirement in 1978.

THE VILLAGE GREEN, NEWTON-ON-TRENT.

The old village green prior to construction of the bypass, once the site of a caravan which was home to eight POWs who worked at Hall Farm.

In March 1946 Hall Farm had eight POWs posted to work on the land who were paid a basic wage of 5s/6d; they also lived in a caravan on the old village green. The POWs began to be repatriated in 1947 and by December 1948 there were only two left, and they chose to stay in this country.

Hall Farm, Newton on Trent (c1902)

Newton has seen its fair share of entertainment and throughout the 1950s concerts and revues were held in the school room in which a lot of the residents performed their own sketches, including Edgar Kyme and Frank Gelder's Burst Pipe sketch. 1950 also saw the opening of The East Midland Sun Folk nudist camp which remains to this day.

In the early 1980s Newton probably saw its biggest change with the construction of the bypass and although this dramatically reduced traffic through the village, it also split part of it across the A57. There was a house occupied by Miss Grimes which the present-day A57 now runs through.

Nowadays Newton has a school (Newton on Trent C of E Primary School, built in 1857), post office & shop, timber merchant and a Christmas shop that opens for November and December.

With its new housing developments and a wide demographic population Newton continues to be an integral part of rural Lincolnshire.

Newton on Trent Timeline

1795 - Flood levels recorded as very high with Newton isolated

1811 - Newton population was 240 of whom 19 were classed as poor

1812 - Newton Hall demolished and Hall Farm built

1818 - The north aisle of the church was demolished and the church 'restored' at the instigation of the infamous Archdeacon of Stow, Dr Cayley Illingworth who ruined many medieval churches in the area

1832 - Dunham Bridge was opened

1837 - Last known reference to Newton on Trent windmill which was believed to have been sold and dismantled

1851 - Census and Religious Survey, Newton population was 336

1855 - The Church of England School (present building) was built

1879 - The Cyclists Touring Club (CTC) was established in 1878 and shortly afterwards The Reindeer public house was named as an approved resting point

1880 - All children must remain at school until 13

1882 - Scarlet fever outbreak at the school

1891 - Newton population was 307

1898 - Mrs Doyle, mother of Sir Arthur Conan Doyle, visited the school accompanied by the vicar's wife, Mrs Stable

1899 - Cinematographic entertainment held in the school on the 17th of January

1900 - Measles epidemic at the school

1915 - A clock was fitted to the church tower

1926 - The Reindeer public house had a 'state of the art' gas generator fitted

The Gelders' shop in Newton on Trent. The family served the village for many years. A residential property now sits where the shop once stood.

1937 - Mains electricity was supplied to Newton on Trent but many houses could not afford it.

1942 - A German bomb landed and exploded behind the bone mill (now the kennels on Dunham Road)

1950 – Gelders' mobile shop began touring the nearby villages

1965 - Mains drainage was installed in Newton

1973 – Kymes' Fish and Chip shop closed down

1979 - New Dunham Bridge was opened

1983 - The village bypass was opened effectively eliminating what was left of the village green.

1990 – Gelders' shop and The Reindeer public house closed. The Groves and Brambles housing developments started

1996 - Stephanie Prosser, the wife of Rev Rhys Prosser, was ordained

2000 - Cockerel's Roost housing development was started. High floods closed Dunham Bridge

2003 - The school trust gained vacant possession of the schoolhouse and garden

School Days

Ex-pupils of Newton on Trent School, Gladys Bayes, Joyce Cupit & Sarah Lidgett, recall what life was like in their school years at Newton on Trent school as they reached their 90th birthdays:

The school then was not just an infant and junior school like it is today, you could stay on at the school until you were 14 at which time you left and started work. It was erected at the expense of Lord Kinloch in 1855.

Gladys recalls how her great uncle, George Clark who was a Newton on Trent man, gave the school to the village in 1921 so that the village would never be without a school. George was born on the 15th April 1857, he used to work for the Grimes' but he later moved away to Sheffield. After talking to two steelwork managers who came to Newton to fish, it is said that despite his love of the country he was 'fired with a desire to come to Sheffield'. In 1882 George Clark founded a steel fabrication company. From his humble origins George Clark became a well-known and much-respected Sheffield figure. He represented Nether Hallam on the city council for 30 years and was made a magistrate in 1928. George died in 1936 but his legacy lives on.

George Clark, who after establishing a successful steel business donated the school buildings to the village of Newton on Trent.

Conditions at the school when the girls were there were very different than they are today. They recall how there was a pump outside for water with little worms in, milk came straight from the cow with complimentary hair! The toilets were also outside (two large and one small one) and there was a wash bowl with some carbolic soap (Lifebuoy) and a very dirty towel to dry your hands on.

There was no electricity and they had oil lamps to help them see. They were kept warm with a coal fire. They recall how Miss Florence Perry was the head teacher and how she was a lovely storyteller, telling stories from books such as Children of the New Forest and Black-Eyed Dennis. As she weaved these magical tales the children got a glimpse of her knee caps so there was only one thing to do, and so they knitted her knee cap covers! Miss Perry lived in the school house with her elderly mother, there was a door from the classroom through to her house so she would set them a test and slip through the door to get her mother some dinner. Gladys remembers how she would wait until she was gone and then they would all look at the answers on her desk.

Newton school photograph 1922. Miss Florence Perry can be seen on the back row on the far left with Miss Doris Kyme on the far right. The Rev Stables can also be seen in the middle of the group.

Sarah Lidgett also recalled how she was very good at mental arithmetic, "You had to answer a question and the person who was the quickest left the classroom first and it was nearly always me," she says, but sometimes she would tell Edgar the answer and he would throw her a sweet!

Edgar's aunty, Miss Doris Kyme, went to the school in 1908, then in 1914 she became a 'Monitress' (a pupil

Monkeys all. The children at Newton School were entertained when a horse arrived with a monkey on its back!

The children of Newton would often put on a show for the villagers. This was the Christmas concert in December 1937.

teacher), and between 1918 and 1969 she was assistant teacher for 51 years. She also ran the Methodist Sunday school for many years and played the harmonium at the chapel.

Miss Perry was the head teacher at the school from 1913 until 1935 and she was followed by Mrs Margery Bingham who was temporary and left after a year. In 1936 the school had another temporary head called Mrs Gladys Peck who left in 1937. In 1940 a Miss Margery Coupe arrived from Leeds with some refugees and they stayed at Hall Farm. Miss Coupe was an assistant teacher at the school but when the children left, Miss Coupe stayed and married an Arthur Moore from Laughterton. In 1946 she became head teacher and moved into the school house. Joyce recalls how a few years ago some evacuees came back to Newton on Trent to see her, Elsie, Edna and Irene Wilson, "It was so lovely to see them again, such a lovely surprise!"

Lots of events went on at the vicarage opposite which was then the residence of Reverend Samuel Stable. Mrs Stable used to run the penny bank at school. Sarah Lidgett remembers dancing round the maypole and having to sit underneath it and hold on to it to keep it from toppling over.

Mr Bacon was the attendance officer and used to come to the school. Miss Perry was very deaf and the children would be chatting away but Mr Bacon used to say "Be quiet children I am not deaf". Gladys laughs and says "I was 14 on the 5th of November and I thought, that's that I've left school, so I went to Wilmot's farm to pick carrots, but Mr Bacon had other ideas and spoke to my mother who told me I had to give up the job and go back to school until Christmas".

The pupils of Newton enjoying the Maypole celebrations in 1933.

Afterschool activities consisted of dancing with Mrs Rees on a Monday night, there were also games to be played like paper chase where you drop paper down for someone else to follow your trail, sometimes this would end up as far a Park Farm! "We used to play all over," says Joyce. Joyce's mother was a dinner lady at the school for two years and so Joyce followed suit and stayed for 32 years, "I enjoyed it so much I didn't want to leave".

A reunion of the school pupils to celebrate the opening of the new extension at Newton School. Pictured left to right are: Babs Minnitt, Frank Sewell, George Sewell, Joyce Cupit, Gladys Bayes, Edgar Kyme, Margaret Veall, Gladys Roper and at the front Margaret Wilmot.

It is wonderful to think that these people have been in each other's lives for so long and no doubt been through a lot together, so it is no wonder great friendships were forged. Joyce and Gladys are still the best of friends and love to reminisce about their school days. "We never argue," say Gladys "We know each other so well."

MY STORY

Bruce Minnitt

Philip Bruce Minnitt - Bruce to his friends - received a letter on 13 March 2010 saying he'd been awarded freedom of the parish. This appeared to be the first such honour in the whole of Lincolnshire.

On 4 September 2010 a plaque was presented to Bruce by Andrew Arden, Chairman of Newton on Trent Parish Council. The plaque was hung in St Peter's Church at Newton on Trent.

Bruce's wife Sylvia Minnitt (née Wilmot), known as Babs,

Bruce cuts a dash in his RAF uniform

was born and raised in Newton while Mr Minnitt was born in Laneham, just over Dunham Bridge. Mr Minnitt first met his wife-to-be when he was standing outside the old blacksmith's in Newton when he saw a group of girls near the telephone kiosk. This first meeting was uneventful and Bruce, just 15 years old, went home sad of heart.

At 17 Mr Minnitt volunteered as a pilot for the RAF. It must have been in his blood as his father, Bernard Minnitt, was a WWI hero, receiving a Military Medal and a Military Cross for service in the battle of the Somme. He died of old age just short of 95 years.

Bruce's new uniform must have had the desired effect because he soon became engaged to his teenage sweetheart. Then, in March 1944, Mr Minnitt was given a short leave because he was due for service in North Africa. He arrived home from where he was stationed in South Wales at 8am on the Saturday and was married by special licence at St Peter's Church, Newton-on-Trent, on the Sunday. The wedding cake was also Babs' 21st birthday cake and the honeymoon was at the Victoria Hotel, Nottingham, the bill for the

two nights being £3 17s 0d.

After 66 years of marriage Mr & Mrs Minnitt are now the oldest living couple in the village. Sadly, some of Bruce's colleagues were not so lucky. One friend, a fellow crew member, who had taken leave at the same time, also to marry by special licence, was never to return home to his new wife.

After Mr Arden presented the plaque, Mr Minnitt made a fine acceptance speech. After thanking Andrew and the parish council for putting his name forward for the award he went on to explain why he thought he may have been nominated. Mr Minnitt had served 52 years on the parish council, from 12 April 1955 to 12 February 2007, during which he has been Vice-chair or Chair for 36 years. He was a school governor for 12 years and a member of the Parochial Church Council for many years.

Bruce and wife Babs take a few moments to pose for the camera

He was a member of the Gainsborough Rural District Council for some years before the local government reorganisation act of 1974 made them all redundant and they were replaced by the newly formed West Lindsey District Council. Among his duties he has seen mains street sewerage arrive at Newton and the erection of old people's flats. He was also district representative on the Lincoln Association of Local Councils and was fortunate in that capacity to be invited, together with his wife, to the Queen's garden party in July 1992.

Bruce continues to live on Newton on Trent where he made his home with Babs all those years ago and despite the village going through a lot of changes over the years it still has a fond place in his heart with many happy memories.

Henry Calvert Grimes

This is a short article about Henry Calvert Grimes, and what we know of his time during the First World War. Born in 1891, Henry Calvert, known as Cal, lived at Hall Farm, Newton on Trent, with his parents Mary and Joseph Grimes and his sister Eleanor. At the age of 19 he joined the Lincolnshire Yeomanry Reserves. Their main barracks were on Burton Road in Lincoln, in what is now the Museum of Lincolnshire Life. The Lincolnshire Yeomanry was formed in 1901 under the Earl of Yarborough and wore a uniform of Lincoln green. Cal trained in the cavalry and took his own horse, a homebred mare called 'The Wren'. Two years later Cal and Wren along with three other troopers, won the section jumping competition.

Once war broke out the 1/1st Lincolnshire Yeomanry was commanded to Egypt. Cal and Wren, along with 450 other troopers and their horses, boarded the troop ship HM Transport Mercian. This journey was anything but plain sailing as an excerpt from a newspaper article in the Lincolnshire Chronicle from Friday 30 April 1971 explains. The headline was 'Horses Were Blown to Pieces and Soldiers' Bodies Cluttered Decks'. The journalist used quotes from Mr H Preston Addey, a fellow trooper in the Lincolnshire Yeomanry. In brief the article read:

It was in November 1915 that the A, B and C squadrons of Lincolnshire Imperial Yeomanry left Southampton for Egypt. HMS Mercian was a coal ship belonging to the Leyland Line of Liverpool and had been specially fitted to take the hundreds of horses belonging to the regiment. She sailed alone completely without escort. Even with three decks there was not enough room to get all the horses under cover and 25 of them were left in open stalls on the top deck.

HMS Mercian used to transport the horses of Lincolnshire Imperial Yeomanry

All went well as far as Gibraltar where they stayed the night. When they started on the second leg of their journey it was a perfect day and many soldiers were on the deck playing bingo when the first sign of trouble came. At 4.30 in the afternoon a shell from a German submarine burst out of the sea over the ship, followed by another which narrowly missed them. That was the start of one-and-a-half hours of shelling with no less than 68 direct hits. Almost the entire crew was lost, including the wheelhouse man which left the ship without a pilot, and all engines had stopped. The regiment was faced with the task of getting the engines going and the ship under way again. This they did, and eventually managed to make some progress. The submarine followed the Mercian for some way into the night, but thinking that

L to R: L Cattle, G Badley, E Barber & HC Grimes at Riseholme

the boat was sinking did not attack again.

The next morning they limped in to Oran harbour in Algeria where they made arrangements for the dead and wounded. With the men lost or wounded in the attack, the regiment had been cut by half in one fell swoop. A fortnight was spent repairing the boat and looking after the remaining horses. By the time they reached Alexandria most of the horses were in a state of collapse.

Once in Egypt, all of 1916 was spent on the Middle East Campaign in Egypt and Palestine fighting the Turks. At times the heat was unbearable and soldiers and horses had long hard days. Towards the end of the war the soldiers of the Lincolnshire Yeomanry had their horses taken away from them and they were ordered to retrain as machine gunners. Henry Calvert was allocated No. 95985. Heartbroken by losing their trusted steeds, they buried their saddlery and spurs in the desert and inscribed an epitaph reading:

Stranger pause and shed a tear
A regiment's heart lies buried here
Sickened and died by no disorder
But broken by a staggering order

Our hearts were warm, theirs as cold as Huns
To take our horses and give us machine guns
For cavalry they said there is no room
So we buried our spurs in a desert tomb

Henry Calvert served in the machine gun corps in France using the Maxim gun until the end of the war. While he was still in France he contracted influenza and was in hospital in Camiers during February 1919. This we know from a letter that the war office wrote to Joseph Grimes, Cal's father.

Henry Calvert was released from actual military duty on 2nd June 1919. He then came home to the farm where he stayed and worked. He remained a keen horseman and was a regular on the hunting field with his horse Blackie. Henry died in 1976 when his granddaughter Alison was 8-years-old, but it has always been known in the family that he hardly ever spoke of his time in the war.

This has been pieced together from information found in an envelope in a drawer in the farmhouse, researched by Hannah Watson, and with information from the Museum of Lincolnshire Life.

NEWTON ON TRENT IN PICTURES

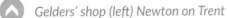

Gelders' shop (left) Newton on Trent

The hunt on the green at Newton on Trent date unknown

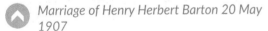

Marriage of Henry Herbert Barton 20 May 1907

Maud Wilmot (on the right) and Kate Wilmot winning 3rd prize of a butter-making competition in the early 1920s.

Children outside the school Newton on Trent 1908.

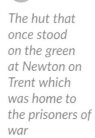

The hut that once stood on the green at Newton on Trent which was home to the prisoners of war

Edgar Kyme & Babs Wilmot as 'The Bride & Groom' in 1931

An aerial view of Newton on Trent. Gelders' shop can still be seen on the right and the area that was once farm buildings behind the shop has now been developed into Orchard Close.

Newton on Trent FC 1936
Back row: Harry Gelder (Snr), Wilf Arden, Len Brown, Jack Stimpson, George Watson, Mr Gourley, Harold Snell, Albert Cottam. Front Row: Tom Wilmot, Harry Gelder (Jnr), Jack Good, ? Hemshall, Jack Sewell, George Clay, Alf Payne.

A group of Morris dancers from Newton on Trent

The bus interchange in Newton on Trent. This was located in the car park of the Reindeer Inn pub which was still open in this picture. The interchange no longer exists and the Reindeer has since become a residential dwelling.

Jimmy Arden's house prior to The Grove development

Cyril Glossop outside his house on the Old High Street

Interior of St Peter's church showing the pews which have since been removed

Maypole dancers in Newton on Trent

The service station which once stood at the end of the High Street in Newton on Trent. The site is now the 'Listers Timber & Builders Merchants' yard

Edgar & Doris Kyme in 1928

The old hall & village, Newton on Trent

Newton Field Day July 18th 1934

Farming in the hay field Newton on Trent in 1931

The Green, Newton on Trent

A group of fishermen on the Trent

The Green   Newton-on-Trent.

A group of likely lads from Newton on Trent, circa 1937.

Pupils say farewell to Mrs Moore

edmistress at Newton-on-Trent Primary School, Mrs. Margery Moore, receives a cut-glass decanter from Mr. Michael Stott.

HEADMISTRESS Mrs. Margery Moore was treated to a surprise presentation last week to mark her retirement from Newton-on-Trent Primary School. Mrs. Moore, of Schoolhouse, Newton-on-Trent, was head teacher for 32 years.

Her first visit to Newton was in 1939 when she arrived with evacuees from Leeds. Although she returned to her home she went to the village for her holidays and eventually married a local lad.

Mr. Michael Stott, Deputy Divisional Education Officer for Lincolnshire County Council, presented Mrs. Moore with a cut glass decanter, and thanked her for her untiring devotion to the school.

Mr. B. Robinson, a former pupil whose children attend the school, presented a garden table, cut glass tumblers, sherry glasses, and a china ornament of two children waving goodbye, on behalf of staff, pupils, parents and friends.

A postcard looking down the High Street towards the church on the right hand side

Newton on Trent Sunday School trip to West Cleethorpes in 1930

A Lincolnshire Echo article on Mrs Moore, headmistress of Newton on Trent school for 32 years on retirement in 1978

A group of children on Newton on Trent High Street, circa 1908. Although the High Street has changed some of the more familiar buildings are still recognisable.

 Newton on Trent concert December 1937

Arthur Arden son of Wilf & Maud Arden c1921

 Mr & Mrs Birkett at the cottage which once stood on Newton Green and has since been demolished.

A view down the High Street with The White Hart (now closed) on the right

A children's fancy dress competition at the Festival of Britain celebrations in Thorney Hall gardens in 1951

THORNEY

Thorney, first mentioned in the Domesday Book as Torneshai, has been recorded under such names as Tunaie, Tiernhoge, Twenhag, Thornehawe, Thornagh, Thornhow, Thornhay and subsequently Thorney.

Introduction

Although a small village comprising some seventy dwellings along the main street and various outlying cottages and farms, there is a fair amount of historical interest associated with this Saxon settlement.

Its roots can be traced back to medieval times when its wood and high forest provided sport for the nobility. (The name Thorney can be translated roughly as that of a 'thorn enclosure'.)

AMONGST THE WOOD AT THORNEY.

Workers including young children in the woods in Thorney circa 1919-1920. The woodlands were an important source of income for the workers & residents of Thorney.

121

VILLAGE TALES

A Brief History

Little is recorded of the early history of the Thorney estate, although it is known that Walter de Clifford handed over patronage of the church of Thorney to Thora, Prioress of Broadholme (a neighbouring village) by way of tax during the third year of the reign of King John. Henry de Lacy, Earl of Lincoln, had free warren (the right to hunt rabbit and game) in Thorney during the reign of Edward I.

About this time, a third of the manor was owned by Fulc le Strange and his wife, Alianora, and was passed to their son, John, at their death during the reign of Edward II.

The rectory of Thorney and the patronage of the village changed hands on the 1st of May 1544, when it was granted to Edward Fynes (Lord of Clinton and Saye) and Robert Tirwhit and their heirs.

It was not until Tudor times that the Thorney estate became established under a sole family name for any length of time. In 1567 the estate was purchased by George Nevile of Ragnall for the sum of £1200 from William Meringe. It was to remain in the Nevile family for the next 300 years or so.

Passages of Time

A bricked-lined tunnel discovered during building work at Thorney Hall caused quite a stir. Below is an excerpt from the Newark Advertiser 16/12/1988

PASSAGES OF TIME
By Dr John Samuels

Nearly every town and village has its stories of secret tunnels. Underground passages connecting church and manor house, church and monastery or even monastery and nunnery.

Sometimes these were said to have been used as an escape route by Roman Catholic priests, or for smugglers or other nefarious activities. Indeed Nottinghamshire can claim one of the most bizarre underground monuments - the Duke of Portland's underground ballroom and connecting railway at Welbeck Abbey. Was he really mad, shy, or just ingenious?

A few weeks ago I had an urgent telephone call that a brick-lined tunnel had been discovered during building work at Thorney Hall. I rushed out there immediately. In the bottom of the old basement to the earlier hall that had been demolished some years ago, was an opening of a tunnel about 3½' wide. Several people had already

crawled along it and reckoned that it was about 40 yards long.

Would I like to go down it myself? No. I have never forgotten being lowered 30ft down an old well which had been discovered in North Lincolnshire. At the bottom I looked up to see the sky as a small circle and the awful thought occurred as to how long it would take to dig me out if the walls collapsed. My opinion was that the tunnel at Thorney Hall was probably for drainage, perhaps to take away excess rainwater that was often stored in old houses for soft water. Then again, it may have been a secret passage to Doddington Hall!

Thorney Hall in 1918, now reduced to all but memories

St Helen's Church

St Helen's parish church was built in 1849/50 after being commissioned by the Reverend Christopher Nevile B A and was consecrated on the 11th April 1850. The previous old Norman church was demolished as the Reverend Nevile believed sincerely that it was of inadequate size for what was to be a developing village.

The modern stone font of St Helen's

St Helen's Church, a mixture of Norman & Romanesque architecture

The construction of the new church reputedly cost £8000 and this, intensified by the agricultural depression, unfortunate investments, three marriages and thirteen surviving children, all helped him to dissipate two fortunes. He died on the 12th August 1877, leaving his third wife a small annual income. His younger brother Charles Nevile M A was the officiating curate of the church.

The church is a standard plan and is a copied combination of Norman and Romanesque architecture, with materials imported from Italy. It was designed by L R Cottingham who is famous for his scripts rather than his edifices.

The west door opens directly into a pleasantly-proportioned nave situated under a timber-pitched roof. The east end points through a semicircular arch into a raised chancel, which has a similar roof to that of the nave.

One of many stone heads found on the church, said to be based on the workers who undertook the construction.

The flooring is a tile mosaic of particular interest. To the left of the nave is the modern stone font with a wooden cover, whilst to the right there is the original Norman font, which is now redundant. Its fragments reveal knot work, foliage and small hardly visible figures, with a plaited band round the rim of the bowl. To the left and right of the aisles are hatchments depicting the Nevile family crest and a stone plaque commemorating one of the Neviles.

The original Norman font, now redundant but preserved inside the church

On the north side of the chancel lies the vestry which had a fireplace installed in 1892 at a cost of £55. The chimney on the outside is disguised by an ornamental dovecote.

In 1988 gales destroyed two of the stained glass windows in the east end of the chancel. Unfortunately, the cost of repairing these windows to their original

The stone arches found at the rear of the church

The roof on the outside is covered with sawn stone. There are two bronze bells on the west wall, only one is operable by pulling a rope on the right of the wooden doorway. The second bell is obsolete.

Behind the church there can be seen two ruined arches and pillars of a mediaeval era.

The iron gates which lead to the entrance of the church were dedicated by the Rector of Thorney, Rev. J R N Tomsen MA in 1935 as a memorial in remembrance of those who gave their life in the First World War.

state would have cost far more than the funds of a small local church would allow. It was with regret that the beautiful chancel was replaced with plate glass, while the one to the north, which was only partially damaged, has been left in place in the hope that a full repair may be affected, if and when funds become available.

The walls of the church are of 'Ashlar' Ancaster stone and embody the normal type of buttresses, parapet and Norman-style windows. The gables of the roof have large coping stones, the tie beams, purlins, roof tree and wall plate are of chestnut and the rafters of the roof boarding are of deal.

The two bronze bells found on the west wall

The Neviles of Thorney

In 1844 we discover that the three townships of Thorney, Wigsley and Broadholme (now known as parishes) comprised of 342 inhabitants and 4140 acres of land, of which 300 were woodland. At that time the manor belonged to the Rev Christopher Nevile, son of Commander Christopher Nevile.

Thorney Hall residence of the Nevile family until 1962

Rev Christopher Nevile appears to have has a flair for finance for in 1865 he received £5000 compensation for allowing the Great Northern Railway to build a new line through his estate.

As previously mentioned in the history of Thorney church, Rev Christopher Nevile dissipated two fortunes within his lifetime which created numerous financial problems for his widow and surviving children. Doubtless it became increasingly difficult to maintain the house and estate on these dwindling resources.

Certainly, the estate had been taken over by Mrs Perry Herrick in 1888 and the name Nevile no longer occurred in the list of electors for the year 1894.

The demise of the Nevile reign in Thorney was almost complete. Indeed the Parish Council Act of 1894 probably accelerated the position, for the villagers began to hold parish meetings with records of meetings appearing in a minutes book of 1896.

Overseers were beginning to be mentioned and were taking over most of the governmental work of the village which had previously been performed by the members of the Nevile family.

After the Great War, during which the hall had been used as a convalescent home, the hall and estate came up for auction and the Neviles returned, intent on buying back their ancestral home and estate. Unfortunately, they were only able to purchase the hall, with most of the estate being sold to local farmers.

Various members of the family resided in the hall periodically between 1918 and 1962. Finally, on Friday the 6th of April 1962 Thorney Hall came under the auctioneers hammer for the last time. The Queen Anne residence was sold and demolished in 1964 to be replaced with a modern building which now stands on the same site. The old servants' quarters have been sympathetically converted into residential dwellings but this is the only part of what was once a magnificent building which still exists.

The Nevile coat of arms which can be found on the wall of St Helen's Church

The Convalescing Soldiers at Thorney Hall

This poem was written by an unknown soldier who stayed at Thorney Hall during the Great War.

How happy am I to have known at all,
Kind sisters and friends at Thorney Hall;
With its stately elm and noble oak,
Who can my happiness provoke.

There are lovely lawns, so green & grand,
With beautiful trees on every hand;
Hurrah for old England, our sea girt strand,
Upon whose shore no foe shall land,

Beside the still waters of yonder pond,
Where we love to fish the whole day long;
And from out of the reeds and rushes so tall,
The moor-hens to their young ones call.

One afternoon I chanced to lie,
Beneath a shady tree close by;
When I heard above a peaceful dove,
Cooing to his mate of love.

Some say the country is quiet and dull,
With nothing at all to break the lull;
But let them remember life would be bright,
If we could always live aright.

Has it ever struck you, as it as me,
This fact with me you will agree;
That people of wealth and leisure combine,
And even prepare for soldiers to dine.

What happy hour I there have spent,
How happy again I there was sent;
So sweet to think of those joyous times,
And in mind to live over many a time.

A Convalescent Soldier

A pair of convalescing soldiers at Thorney Hall

The Old Manor House

One of the oldest-dated brick houses in Nottinghamshire, the Manor of Thorney was bought by George Nevile of Grove in 1567. In this sense, 'manor' meant estate rather than house. The house currently called The Old Manor was probably built by George Nevile of Aubourn (where the Nevile family still lives) or by his second son and namesake in around 1649, the date prominently displayed in a terracotta plaque on the north front of the house. A much-eroded plaque in the west gable displays the faint initials GN.

The Old Manor House prior to its restoration and in a state of some disrepair

The terracotta plaque showing the build date as 1649

The house as built would not have been intended for George Nevile to live in, since his residence was situated some 500 yards to the south where its successor, Thorney Hall, once stood. Rather, The Old Manor, with its old-fashioned form and typical Nottinghamshire 3-cell-plan was probably built to house the estate steward or principal farmer, with a west-facing parlour at one end of the house (on the right of the photograph) for the steward and his wife. A hall or 'housebody', centrally placed, still retains a broad inglenook cooking hearth and beyond, a cold larder at the east end. The date plaque of 1649 records the year of the execution of Charles I. This would have been an important, if doleful, commemoration for the Nevile family which was staunchly Royalist in the Civil War. A second date plaque, reset over the garden gate to the property, records the birth of a Nevile heir in 1662.

Latterly the house, which in all probability would have housed farm workers in addition to the steward and his family, (there are two main bedchambers on the first floor and a large landing or 'pass chamber' between them over the hall, as well as two attic chambers) was divided into two cottages and known as Manor (or Hall) Cottages which, when they were restored as a single dwelling after the estate was sold up in the 1960s, became known (erroneously) as The Manor House.

When an RAF officer and his wife restored the house in 1972-4, a farmer returned one of the stone balls that decorated the apex of each gable and, in a more recent restoration, the sole of a child's shoe was found hidden in the hall fireplace bressumer beam. Such hidden objects were supposed to ward off evil. In recent work in the front garden, 17th century pottery sherds and clay pipe bowls have been found, proving that a busy domestic life was carried on down Mill Lane, with barns and farm buildings, including a sawmill, surrounding this substantial but not grand old house.

It has been said that The Old Manor is the oldest dated brick house in Nottinghamshire. Whilst technically this may be true, the form of the brick window mullion in the (undated) brick house in Kneesall suggests that it is a good 50 years earlier than The Old Manor which, whilst displaying some Elizabethan characteristics (projecting plinth, moulded string course, pedimented window, Tudor arched doorway) is firmly tied to its mid-17th century date by the presence of its 1649 date plaque.

The Old Manor House in 2011. After 10 years of care & attention from its current owners it has been restored to its former glory including a traditional knot garden

Thorney School

The school was built by the Nevile family. Naturally because of the size of the village, it was only a small school and had accommodation for fifty-four children. Originally it was called the Thorney Church of England School.

Its logbook dates back to October 12th 1900 when the weekly average attendance at the school was approximately 18 children. The vicar of the parish, a Mr J Smith, visited the school very frequently and they always had monthly examinations!

A few interesting facts are noted in the logbook which are worthy of mention. The children were given holidays for potato picking and during the season many children did not attend school because they were 'blackberrying'. The majority of the children lived quite a distance from the school so that on one rainy day only eleven children arrived for the morning session.

Thorney was an all-age school at this time, as was exemplified on the 17th November 1902 when a girl was admitted who was 13 years 7 months, and a boy entered the school only just over three-years-old. At this time the teacher was getting sixty pounds per annum.

Three people now visited the school quite frequently, we are told in 1903. These people are the Vicar of Thorney, an HMI and the Attendance Officer. The reason for the frequency of visits was that the HMI was not satisfied with the standard of teaching in the school so in 1904 another head teacher, Sarah Ann Stawland took over.

From the logbook we also learn that during the First World War Thorney Hall was used as a convalescent home for soldiers and in 1915 a number of these soldiers actually visited the school to talk to the children and see what work they were doing.

In 1940 there were twenty-five children on the books and in 1946 only seventeen, although in 1949 the numbers had risen again to twenty-seven. On the 25th April of that same year the seniors were transferred to Harby School. Then on August 29th 1951 when Broadholme School was closed, fifteen children along with the school equipment were transferred to Thorney, which made the number on the books up to forty.

Miss Vera Mary Harrison BA, Headmistress of Broadholme C of E School, was appointed Headmistress of Thorney School and a private coach took the children to Thorney at 9am and took them home at 3.30pm.

Thorney School children in 1923. Teacher Aggie Barber can be seen on the far left

In 1954 the school's face was given an uplift and many improvements were made. The building was decorated, electric lighting fitted and the playground received a new surface, but on the 1st October 1958 the school received official notification that it was to be closed in due course. So on the 25th March 1959 when the school closed for the Easter holidays it also terminated its life as a school.

Mr Nevile of Thorney Hall had actually received a letter from J Edward Mason the Minister of Education for Nottinghamshire, stating that he had given permission for the school to be closed.

After the Easter holidays the children began to attend Harby Queen Eleanor School, in fact there was a complete transfer of children and staff from Thorney to Harby School.

After closure in 1959 Thorney School retained its importance in village life when it became a village hall for the community. It remained at the centre of community life until approximately 2003 when it finally closed and was sold by the Church of England. It is now a residential dwelling.

 *A collection of children at Thorney Sunday School in 1920*

MY STORY

Rachel Stow

My parents, Tom and Mary Payne, married in 1936 and moved to Thorney to start their married life. They went on to have four children, Thomas, John, Rachel (myself) and Geoffrey, and lived in Thorney until moving to Laughterton in 1967.

They lived in what was then known as The Old Vicarage, which is situated opposite the first two council houses (however these were built at a later

The Old Vicarage, home to Rachel's family

date). They had a poultry farm on their premises and for a while my father rented Hawthorn Farm. The Old Vicarage has since been converted into three dwellings.

Thorney High Street originally was home to a post office which the gentleman in this picture can be seen walking towards

For many years a garden fete was held on the tennis court that was situated at the front of the house. These occasions always took place on Whit Monday and attracted people from both the village and the surrounding area. In fact one year a family came from Skegness! Attractions included Bowling for a Pig (a real life pig!), Skittles, Penny in a Pancheon, Spinning Wheel, Ski Ball and Hoopla. Refreshments were provided – sandwiches, cakes and cups of tea. There was always either a fancy dress or a decorated cycle/pram competition. The Whit Monday garden fete was held for a great number of years and only

one wet day can be recalled when proceedings were moved rather swiftly into the village hall. Despite my father's insistence that the charges of the fete should be kept affordable to all, the fete always generated a considerable income which went towards the upkeep of the church and the village hall.

The Old Vicarage also had a tennis court. On Whit Monday this would also host the fete for which people came from miles around.

As mentioned, a tennis court was situated at the front of the house and during the summer months many people from the village came to play tennis on a Tuesday and Friday evening. These evenings were always fun with much banter and friendly competition and on a Friday evening the ice cream van came into the village and a threepenny (3d) cornet or wafer was enjoyed by both players and spectators alike.

The village boasted a church, a village school (which later became the village hall) and a post office-cum-general store. The post office/general store was run by Mrs Turner and later by her daughter, Edie. Myself and my brothers remember going into the general store with our ration books. Edie was also the church organist.

All of the children attended the village school – in those days you started at the age of five at the local school and remained there throughout your schooldays which finished at the age of fifteen. At one point there was only one teacher, Mrs Key from Saxilby, she was later joined by Mrs Talks. When Broadholme School closed the children from there came to Thorney and Mrs Harrison became Head Teacher. By this time there was secondary education and at 11 we went to Harby Secondary School. Eventually Collingham Wood Hill Secondary School opened and we went there. Anyone passing their 11 plus went to either Lincoln or Newark.

My Mum helped at the Sunday school and each year we had an outing to the

A Sunday school outing (around 1951)

seaside (a very big treat in those days!). We were given a little bit of spending money – the amount depended on your attendance at Sunday school throughout the previous year. Each child was also given a packet of crisps – again a treat especially to have a whole packet to yourself! The venue for the outing rotated each year between Skegness, Mablethorpe and Cleethorpes. My favourite was Skegness.

The local church remains an impressive building to this day and was the venue for my wedding in 1966. When I was growing up the mainstay of the church was a lady called Mrs Nevile who lived in and owned Thorney Hall. Since that time part of the hall has been demolished and a new dwelling has been built on the site.

 A school photograph taken in approximately 1948, do you recognise anyone?

THORNEY IN PICTURES

Thorney sawmill in 1928

A reinforced water tank crashes to the ground . . . and another part of Thorney Hall is demolished. Mr. H. A. Bonning, the new owner, is pulling down the 40-roomed hall, built in 1750, and building a new house on the site.

 An early drawing of Thorney Hall, date unknown

 This newspaper article documents the final demise of Thorney Hall

 Fir Farm cottage where Tom Hardy, Thorney resident, lived & his family (& his family before that) lived

Aggie Barber, Edith Turner & the Revd Bestwick in 1923

Mr & Mrs Tom Clarke, residents of Thorney along with their 10 children!

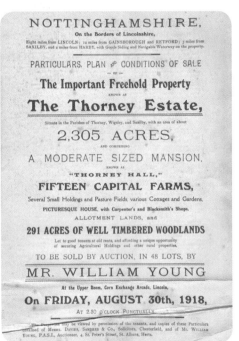

Details of the sale of Thorney estate in 1918

Between 1885 and 1948 little change can be seen on the maps however note that in 1185 Thorney was in Nottinghamshire and in 1948 it was in Lincolnshire.

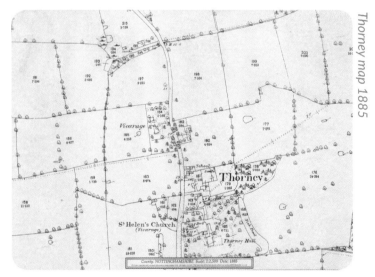

Thorney map 1885

Thorney Hall was up for sale again in 1962, this time broken into lots and this would be the last time it changed hands before it was demolished

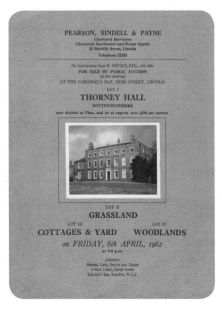

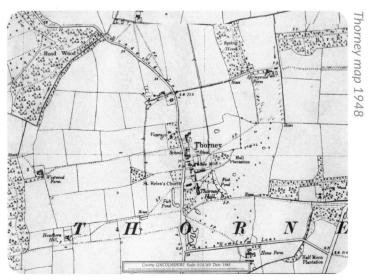

Thorney map 1948

Residents in fancy dress in 1939

All that remains of Thorney Hall are the servants quarters now converted to residential dwellings. You can see the new house that was built to the far right

Cottages on Main Street, Thorney in 1918

Thorney Football Club, 1919-1920

Workers at Thorney Woods in 1920

TORKSEY

Torksey is a small village in the West Lindsey district of Lincolnshire. It is situated seven miles south of Gainsborough and nine miles north-west of the city of Lincoln.

GREA

Torksey Station and guards. See page 147 for full story

VILLAGE TALES

Torksey War Memorial

The following men are mentioned on the WW1 memorial in St Peter's Church, Torksey:
Information researched by David Ingleby of Torksey.

CHARLES HENRY FROW

PRIVATE 241773, 5TH BATTALION
THE YORKSHIRE REGIMENT
KILLED IN ACTION 23RD APRIL 1917

John Frow was born in Kirton in Lindsey where he married Harriet Rowbottom in 1880. He worked as a signalman for the Great Central Railway and by 1882 they had moved to Torksey where their first four children were born. There was then a brief stay in Gainsborough before the family returned to Torksey.

Charles was the fourth child of six, born in 1887 and we know he was working by the age of 14 as in 1901 he is working as a groom at Brampton, probably for a local farmer. However, by April 1911, he had moved to Bridlington in the East Riding of Yorkshire where he had found work as a grocer's assistant.

He lived in a boarding house on the Promenade owned by a local man, William Atkin. Three of William and his wife's eleven children lived with their parents, one being 25-year-old Harriet Atkin.

Later in 1911 Charles and Harriet married, moving to a property further along the Promenade. I have not traced any children born to the marriage.

His Army service record has not survived and we know he didn't arrive in France until after January 1st 1916 having enlisted at Doncaster, as he was not eligible for the 1915 Star. He had originally been in the Royal Field Artillery, but at some stage was transferred to the Yorkshire Regiment. His new battalion had been in France since the 17th of April 1915 so Charles would have been part of a draft of reinforcements.

In May 1915 the battalion had become part of 150th Brigade, 50th (Northumbrian) Division, which, in 1916, fought at the same three actions on the Somme, as did George Denman's brigade – Flers-Courcelette, Morval and Le Transloy. Whether Charles took part in these actions we do not know.

Charles would, however, have been present at the outset of the Battle of Arras in Spring 1917. As is the case with many of the major battles of the First World War, the Battle of Arras was made up of many actions in the vicinity of the French town. The fighting started on April 9th and extended through to the middle of June. Initial success soon gave way to the usual attritional slog with many, many casualties.

The first advances were made around the valley of the River Scarpe. 50th Division took part in the first Battle of The Scarpe from April 9th to 14th but the 5th Yorkshire Regiment was not involved, being in billets at Liencourt and Lattre-St-Quentin.

On the 12th they marched to Arras itself and went into the complex of chalk caves that burrowed under the town and which became a major staging post for troops taking part in the offensive. They are now open to the public and provide a fascinating insight to how the caves were transformed into an underground army base.

On the 15th of April they moved out into the former German frontline trenches that had been captured, moving into Nepal Trench on the 19th in readiness for the action that followed.

The battalion's war diary for April 23rd reads:

Offensive operations. At 4.45am the battalion moved up in support of the 4th East Yorkshire Regt., who were attacking. Reinforcements were supplied during the advance and the whole battalion was brought up to meet the counter attack, which had succeeded in forcing back our troops to their original front line. Here the battalion held the line until 6.00pm when a second attack was launched in conjunction with 2 battalions of the 141st Brigade. This attack was successful and the line gained was held all night.

The battalion was relieved on the next day (the 24th) and moved to the reserve trenches before moving to their billets in Arras.

A note in the column after the war diary note details the battalion's casualties:

Killed	3 officers and 15 other ranks
Wounded	5 officers and 118 other ranks
Missing	2 officers and 55 other ranks
Died of wounds	1 other rank

Sadly Charles was one of the fifteen other ranks to die in the action. He is buried in Heninel Communal Cemetery Extension, in the village of Heninel, near Arras. The village was captured in the first Battle of The Scarpe on the 12 of April and the 50th Division's Burial Officer started the cemetery extension in the same month. Charles lies with twenty-eight fellow members of his regiment.

FRED WALKER BAINES

STOKER FIRST CLASS ROYAL NAVY K24662 (PORTSMOUTH)
DIED OF ILLNESS DECEMBER 10TH 1916

Fred was born in Ragnall, Nottinghamshire on October 1st 1886, the youngest child and only son of Samuel and Lucy Baines. Five years after Fred's birth, Samuel was working as a farm labourer at Laneham near Retford.

Ten years later we find the Torksey connection as Samuel had moved to find work in the village where he was described as a farm foreman. Fred is the only child still living at home, but even at the age of fourteen he had left school and was working as a farm waggoner.

We do not know when exactly they moved to Torksey, but it was after April 1901 and Fred had left the village by early April 1911 as he is working as a coal miner and living with a relation in Anston, near Sheffield. His parents, however, remained in the village and it was natural that they would want to remember their only son on the local memorial.

In late 1911, Fred married Rhoda J Ash in the Rotherham area. Two children were born, Lucy E in the autumn of 1912 and Fred L in late 1913. A double bout of tragedy was to strike Fred as his wife Rhoda died in early 1914 (perhaps from complications from the birth of their second child) and young Fred died in early 1915, leaving just Fred and his young daughter Lucy.

It was at this sad time that Fred joined the Royal Navy. He was twenty-eight years old, 5' 8" tall with light brown hair, grey eyes and a fresh complexion. He had been in the wars as he is described as having a long scar on the right hand side of his forehead, scars on the bridge of his nose and on the outside of his right eye, and had a 'coal' scar on his left forearm – perhaps coloured by the coal dust.

After an initial spell of training at the shore base HMS Victory II, he was posted in July 1915 as a stoker to HMS Lily, a newly-built sloop built for minesweeping. Two months later he was transferred back to HMS Victory II before a spell on HMS Canada that lasted until May 1916.

This ship was a Dreadnought battleship originally intended for sale to Chile, but placed into service with the Royal Navy immediately on her completion. HMS Canada took part in the major naval battle of the First World War at Jutland, but Fred had left the ship just a month before for a further spell at HMS Victory II where he stayed until September 1916.

He then received his last posting to the newly-built HMS Renown, which was the lead ship of her class of battlecruisers. She had been launched on March 4th 1916 and completed on September 20th 1916. She served with the Grand Fleet in the North Sea during the remaining two years of the First World War. Renown was assigned to the 1st Battlecruiser Squadron for the duration of the war, but never fired a shot in anger.

 HMS Renown

I believe Fred fell ill while on board HMS Renown and was transferred to two hospital ships based at Scapa Flow. His official record shows a transfer from Renown to Victory II, the shore base at Portsmouth on December 4th 1916 but this would have been for purely administrative purposes.

The name of the first hospital ship is illegible (see later), but the second was HMS Agadir. This ship was requisitioned in 1914 by the Admiralty for use as a Grand Fleet Hospital Ship at Scapa Flow and was returned to her owners in 1918.

There is some confusion in the records as to his actual condition. The Naval Service Record indicates septicaemia. However, I have traced a letter written to his daughter by the Fleet Surgeon on board what looks like Hospital Ship 'Sondaw' (I have not found a ship of that name) dated December 7th 1916. It reads:

"Dear Madam

I am writing to inform you that your father, Frederick W Baines, Stoker, HMS Renown, was admitted to this Hospital Ship on the 3rd of December. His symptoms

point to Enteric Fever and today his condition had become much worse. You can rest assured that everything possible is being done for him. There is no disguising the fact, however, that he is very seriously ill and in danger of losing his life. I will keep you informed of his progress.

Yours faithfully,
Charles V Wordwright
Fleet Surgeon
Senior Medical Officer"

Enteric fever is another name for typhoid, a totally different condition to septicaemia. Equally the letter is written to his daughter, yet this is 1916 and she was only four years old. She was an orphan and presumably living with relatives, but it seems a bit stark for the Navy to write to a young child who would remember little of her parents.

Sadly, Fred did not respond to treatment and he died of septicaemia just six days later. He is buried at Lyness Royal Naval Cemetery on the Orkney island of Hoy, close to the Scapa Flow Naval Base.

GEORGE WILLIAM DENMAN

DRIVER 72362, 87TH (HOWITZER) BATTERY
12TH BRIGADE ROYAL FIELD ARTILLERY
DIED OF WOUNDS 23RD OCTOBER 1918

George William was born in Torksey in 1890, the youngest child of George and Elizabeth. Both parents and some of his siblings were born in Nottinghamshire. The family moved to Torksey some time between 1876 and 1878 and George senior found work as a riverside labourer before becoming an agricultural labourer. In 1901, Elizabeth is shown as an osier peeler.

Between 1901 and 1911 George William left the family home and moved to Great Houghton, near Barnsley, where he lodged with a local family and found work as a coal miner.

His service record has not survived, but we know that he was a Driver (they 'drove' the teams of horses pulling the guns) in the Royal Field Artillery's 12th (Howitzer) Brigade.

This brigade of the Royal Field Artillery was a unit of Britain's pre-war regular army and comprised 43, 86 & 87 (Howitzer) Batteries. It was sent to France with 6th Division in September 1914. We know from George's medal roll index card that he landed in France (probably as part of a draft of reinforcements) on August 18th 1915.

The Brigade was broken up in May 1916 and 87 (Howitzer) Battery less a section was transferred to 2nd Brigade, part of 6th Division.

George's new brigade acted as part of the 6th Division's Divisional Artillery, and would have seen action throughout the last three months of 1916 during The Battle of the Somme, incorporating the individual actions at Flers-Courcelette, Morval and Le Transloy.

In 1917, the brigade would have fought at the Battle of Hill 70, a Canadian-led assault near Lens in France aimed at diverting German troops from the fierce fighting around Ypres, and later in the Cambrai operations where the tank saw its first major action.

The last year of the war saw the brigade almost continually engaged. They started at the Somme at the Battle of St Quentin in March 1918. This was part of the German's immense blanket attack across much of the Western Front in their final, but ultimately unsuccessful, throw of the dice to try and break the Allied lines.

The Ypres Salient was their next destination with the

brigade taking part in the Battle of Bailleul, where the town was reduced to rubble by the ferocity of the German artillery fire. From here, they again tried to resist the German advance in the two battles of Kemmel Ridge and the subsequent push back in Flanders.

They were then transferred back to the Somme to take part in the battles of the Hindenburg Line – the beginning of the end of German fighting power as the Allies started their push for victory.

Here the brigade fought in the battles of Epehy (September 18th), St Quentin Canal (29th September – 2nd October), Beaurevoir (3-5 October) and Cambrai again (8-9 October).

It is impossible to confirm exactly when and where George received the wounds that would ultimately cause his death. We do know from his entry in the Army Registers of Soldiers' Effects that he died at the No.5 General Hospital in Rouen, a base hospital well behind the lines and close to the Channel ports if casualties needed repatriation. The town housed seventeen major hospitals and convalescent depots.

George died of his wounds on October 23rd, so it is likely he was wounded as part of the fighting on the Somme as the Allies began to push the Germans back. He is buried in the massive St Sever Cemetery Extension in Rouen, which contains over 8,300 burials.

LEIGH HURST

PRIVATE 240129, 4TH BATTALION, THE LINCOLNSHIRE REGIMENT
KILLED IN ACTION APRIL 29TH 1918

Leigh was born in Torksey in 1895, the son of John and Elizabeth Hurst. John had worked as a sand labourer (presumably in the sand quarry), and then as a labourer at the Torksey golf course, which had been the home of the Lincoln Golf Club since 1903. Indeed, Leigh himself worked there as a golf caddie in the 1911 census.

We know little of Leigh between 1911 and the war years, but we know that he was hauled up before the Lindsey magistrates in 1908, aged 13, for selling adulterated milk in the village. Apparently Leigh bought the milk himself and sold it for his own profit. Sadly the milk was reported as being 11% deficient of fat and Leigh was fined 2s 6d and 4s 6d costs.

From his service number, it is possible that Leigh joined the Lincolnshire Regiment before the outbreak of war. His original service number of 1492 is certainly of pre-war issue, but the Territorial Force numbering was changed in 1917 and Leigh's number changed to that shown above.

The 4th Lincolnshire Battalion was originally formed in April 1908 out of the two volunteer battalions of the regiment. In 1915 it was formed into the 46th (North Midland) Division and landed at Le Havre on March 1st 1915, Leigh included.

In January 1916 the battalion moved to Egypt, turning round and returning to France almost immediately. On January 31st 1918 the battalion was moved into the 59th (2nd North Midland) Division but was reduced to cadre strength on May 8th 1918 after suffering heavy casualties.

The 46th (North Midland) Division saw action at a number of places before 1918 such as the Germans liquid fire attack at Hooge and the assault on the Hohenzollern Redoubt (both in 1915), the disastrous diversionary attack at Gommecourt on the first day of the Somme assaults in 1916 and a number of actions in 1917.

After the 4th Lincolnshires were transferred to the 59th (2nd North Midland) Division, they took over the front line at Bullecourt in early February 1918. They were soon on the receiving end of the massive German attacks across the whole Western Front in March 1918, designed to cut the Allies' lines.

The 4th Lincolnshires were in the way of the German onslaught and fought tenaciously at the Battles of St Quentin (21st/22nd March) and Bailleul (15th April). At this point the battalion was reduced in strength from four to two companies. More was to follow with heavy casualties being sustained at the First Battle of Kemmel Ridge on April 17th.

All told, between March 21st and April 17th, the battalion suffered massive casualties with seven officers and forty-one other ranks being killed, ten officers and two hundred and thirty-six other ranks wounded and one officer and two hundred and twenty-eight other ranks reported as missing. A total of seven hundred and twenty-three men were posted as killed, wounded or missing.

Amazingly, Leigh survived the slaughter, at least for a few days. The battalion's war diary entry for the date of his death, April 29th 1918, reads:

The morning was quiet but in the evening the enemy obtained direct hits in the camp, which was immediately evacuated. Casualties: KILLED 4 OTHER RANKS, WOUNDED 8 OTHER RANKS

Shell slits were dug in and adjacent field and Battalion HQ was established at the 2nd/4th Leicesters Regt. HQ on the invitation of Lt. Col. Colquhoun DSO.

Leigh was one of the four men killed that day and he lies, with his battalion comrades, in Bailleul Communal Cemetery Extension. As Bailleul was occupied by the Germans after the Spring Offensive of 1918 through to August 1918, the cemetery was enlarged and rebuilt afterwards as many plots had been damaged or lost by bombing. After the Armistice, graves in four other cemeteries were concentrated in the new extension.

SIDNEY FREDERICK JUBB

PRIVATE 46487, 13TH BATTALION
YORK & LANCASTER REGIMENT
KILLED IN ACTION 12TH APRIL 1918

He was known in the family as Fred and born at Torksey in March 1899. His father George worked as a waggoner on a local farm in the village and his mother was employed as an osier peeler. Fred would follow his two elder brothers into service with the Great Central Railway (almost certainly at Torksey Station) as porters.

Fred signed up for Army service a day before his eighteenth birthday on March 21st 1917, but was not called up until May of that year. At the time he was nearly 5' 9" tall and weighed over nine and a half stone.

He spent much of his early time training with various elements of the West Yorkshire Regiment moving between various UK training camps. He was reprimanded and confined to barracks for three days in November 1917 for having a dirty mess tin at the time of a kit inspection!

He was transferred on completion of his training to the 13th Battalion of the York and Lancaster Regiment on March 30th 1918 (known as the Barnsley Pals) and joined his regiment in Belgium three days later.

This battalion had been on the Western Front since March 1916.

In early April the division was heavily involved in trying to stem the advance of the German army's Spring Offensive and, on April 12th and 13th, it formed part of the British line protecting the town of Hazebrouck, close to the Franco/Belgian border.

Although the battalion's war diary is not available, it seems clear that Sidney was killed on the opening day of the Battle of Hazebrouck, just ten days after joining his battalion. Interestingly, it seems official notification of his death was received by the British authorities from an official German list of the dead and accepted in January 1919. Perhaps he had been posted as missing in the first instance. His mother was awarded a pension initially of 7s 4d per week, but this was reduced to 5/- per week from December 17th 1918.

Sadly, his body was never found or identified and he is commemorated on Ploegsteert Memorial (Plugstreet to the British Army). The memorial commemorates over 11,000 men of the British and South African forces who fought in this area during the war.

ARTHUR LISTER

PRIVATE 24611, 2ND BATTALION
THE GRENADIER GUARDS
KILLED IN ACTION 26TH SEPTEMBER 1916, AGED 25

Born in early 1891, Arthur was the son of William and Ellen Sophia Lister. William farmed at Castle Farm in the village. Arthur was to lose both his parents in a relatively short space of time, Ellen in 1902 and William in 1905.

The 1911 census shows Arthur as a grocer living with a widow (a self-employed pork butcher) and her daughter, as a boarder in a property in Burton Road, Lincoln. Perhaps it was at the Co-Operative store in Burton Road.

Sadly, his army service record has not survived, but we know from his medal roll index card that he didn't serve abroad until after the beginning of 1916.

The 2nd Battalion of the Grenadier Guards was a pre-war regular army unit and had landed at Le Havre on August 15th 1914 and had been on the Western Front continuously. As part, initially, of 2nd Division they had seen action continuously through 1914 (Mons, Marne, Aisne and Ypres) and had fought at the Battle of Festubert in 1915.

The battalion was then transferred to the newly-formed Guards Division and saw action at the Battle of Loos, also in 1915. Their next action was on the Somme in 1916.

They were not involved in the first two-and-a-half months of the campaign, but were introduced to the action at the Battle of Flers-Courcelette, between September 15th and 22nd. After weeks of attritional fighting, this was a large-scale offensive designed to take the German's third line of defence and brought names such as Pozieres, High Wood, Delville Wood and Guillemont to the nation's attention for the first time.

It was also notable for the first introduction into the fray of the tank – albeit in small numbers. It was not to be until the following year that they were deployed in numbers. The battle was successful in achieving its aims and a deep advance was made.

Flers-Courcelette was immediately followed by the Battle of Morval (25th–28th September), which saw the army move into flatter, more open ground with some severe fighting. However, the advance continues as the weather started to turn with rain making the battlefield difficult and heralding the quagmire it became later.

On the 25th, the Guards Division attacked with two brigades in line, which advanced in waves 75 yards apart. A German counter-barrage began on the Guards Division front, within a minute of the infantry advancing but the leading waves moved fast enough to avoid the bombardment. The foremost battalions of the 1st Guards Brigade found little opposition, apart from uncut wire, which was cut by the officers, while the men provided covering fire and fire from dug-outs along a sunken road on the extreme right flank. The first objective was rushed at 12.40pm and captured by 1.20pm. The advance to the next

objective took ten minutes, against 'slight' opposition and the advance to the final objective was conducted against little resistance, the right-hand brigade digging-in on the east side of Lesboeufs by 3.30pm.

The battalion Commanding Officer, in his report to the Divisional HQ, said of the 26th:

"Sniping and shelling continued all night (25th) and next morning (26th). During the afternoon of the 26th we were heavily shelled. The Germans could be seen counter-attacking about half a mile to our left and also digging in along the ridge to our front.

...... The dash and gallantry of the Infantry was magnificent in spite of large numbers of recent drafts and totally untrained men being in the ranks (perhaps including Arthur?), but the co-operation of the Artillery was remarkable for its absence and a great deal of ammunition was uselessly expended on ground where no Germans were, and places where Germans could be seen were left untouched."

Casualties were horrendous. Between the 13th to 16th September (Flers-Courcelette) the battalion lost three officers (killed or died of wounds) with nine wounded and 96 other ranks killed, sixteen died of wounds, 232 wounded and thirteen missing. On the 25th and 26th of September in the fighting in and around Lesboeufs, the battalion lost four officers killed with five wounded and sixty-seven other ranks killed, eleven who died of wounds, 175 wounded and 77 missing. Over seven hundred men killed, wounded or missing.

Arthur was one of those killed on the 26th, presumably in the shelling. Was he one of the totally untrained men who had recently joined the battalion? He is buried in the appropriately named Guard's Cemetery at Lesboeufs, about ten miles from Albert.

At the time of the Armistice, the cemetery consisted of only 40 graves (now Plot I), mainly those of officers and men of the 2nd Grenadier Guards who died on the 25th September, but it was very greatly increased when graves were brought in from the battlefields and small cemeteries round Lesboeufs.

There are now 3,137 casualties of the First World War buried or commemorated in this cemetery. 1,644 of the burials are unidentified but there are special memorials to 83 soldiers known or believed to be buried among them.

GEORGE LISTER

YEOMAN SIGNALLER HMS CHATHAM
KILLED IN ACTION 31ST MAY 1916, AGED 28

Born April 5th 1888, George was the son of William and Ellen Sophia Lister, who we have met with his younger brother Arthur. William farmed at Castle Farm in the village. George was to lose both his parents in a relatively short space of time, Ellen in 1902 and William in 1905. Arthur was also to die in the First World War.

George had joined the Royal Navy in July 1903 as a boy trainee and served at a number of shore-based training bases. On his eighteenth birthday, he became a Signaller on board HMS Resolution, signing on for an engagement of twelve years. He was already 5 feet 8 inches tall and was working as a farm-hand. He had brown hair, light hazel eyes and a fresh complexion.

He served on a number of ships, slowly rising up the ranks and earning good or very good conduct ratings. In the 1911 census he is serving on HMS Alert as a Leading Signaller. He served on this ship from February 1910 to November 1911. He was also passed as being educationally qualified for a petty officer and on December 5th 1912 he was appointed Yeoman Signaller.

At the outbreak of war he was serving on HMS Commonwealth, attached to the 3rd Battle Squadron and assigned to the Grand Fleet. The squadron was used to supplement the Grand Fleet's cruisers on the Northern Patrol. On 2 November 1914, the squadron was detached to reinforce the Channel Fleet and was rebased at Portland. It returned to the Grand Fleet on 13 November 1914.

Further shore-based assignments followed until, on May 2nd 1916, he was transferred to HMS Chester, a Town-class light cruiser of the Royal Navy. The ship was laid down on 7 October 1914, launched on 8 December 1915 and entered service in May 1916, three weeks before the Battle of Jutland.

Before the battle HMS Chester was attached to Rear-Admiral Hood's battlecruiser squadron. This unit was normally part of Admiral Beatty's battlecruiser fleet, but just before the battle it had been sent to Scapa Flow for gunnery practise, and so was with the Grand Fleet.

As Admiral Hood approached the battlecruiser battle, the Chester was five miles to his west, on his starboard flank), placing her nearest to the battle. At 5.27 Captain Lawson heard gunfire and went to investigate, running into the German 2nd Scouting Group.

The German cruisers opened fire on the Chester, and inflicted heavy damage on her – three of her $5\frac{1}{2}$in guns were destroyed, as was her aft control station. She was hit by 17 small projectiles, and suffered heavy casualties – 35 dead and 42 wounded. She escaped by fleeing back towards Admiral Hood's battlecruisers, and in the short battle that followed the German cruiser Wiesbaden was so badly damaged that she later sank.

HMS CHESTER

Seventeen 150mm shells hit HMS Chester with 29 men killed and 49 wounded with many of the wounded losing legs because the open backed gun-shields did not reach the deck and give adequate protection. Amongst the gun crew fatalities was 16-year-old John Cornwell who received the Victoria Cross for his dedication to duty though mortally injured.

George was one of those killed and buried at sea. He is remembered on the Chatham Naval Memorial, and also on a memorial in Chester Cathedral that remembers the ship and its casualties.

 HMS Chester

EDWARD NELSON

LANCE CORPORAL S/8761, 9TH (PIONEER) BATTALION
THE GORDON HIGHLANDERS
KILLED IN ACTION APRIL 8TH 1917, AGED 23

Edward is a bit confusing as he also appears to have been known at times as William, or both Edward and William. His birth was registered in 1894, the son of Edward Moody Nelson and his wife Annie. Edward senior had been born at Driffield in the East Riding of Yorkshire, but had evidently moved to Lincoln by 1893 when the couple married. In 1911 they were living in New Boultham Avenue and Edward senior worked as a joiner at an engineering works. By January 1915 they had moved to Webb Street.

Edward was one of eleven children of which seven had survived by the time of the 1911 census. However, he appears at some stage to have become the 'adopted' child of the vicar of Torksey, the Reverend Alfred William Lazenby. This appears to have taken place after Edward's enlistment on January 15th 1915 as his address is given c/o of The Vicarage in Torksey and his father's name is crossed out and Lazenby's name inserted as next of kin.

It is unlikely we will ever know why this is so and it does beg the question of how Alfred Lazenby met Edward and what prompted him to become his 'adopted father'.

Edward was employed as an engineer when he enlisted

The 9th (Service) Battalion of the Gordon Highlanders was formed in Scotland in September 1914 as part of Kitchener's 2nd New Army, and in January 1915, it became the Regiment's Pioneer Battalion.

Following Edward's enlistment in January 1915 it moved to two UK-based training depots before landing at Boulogne on July 9th 1915. It was part of the 15th (Scottish) Division, which took part in the Battle of Loos in 1915, several actions within the Battle of the Somme in 1916 and was heavily involved in the Arras Offensive of April 1917.

He was promoted to Lance Corporal on June 7th 1915. On September 4th 1916, during the Battle of the Somme, Edward was admitted by Field Ambulance to the 34th Casualty Clearing Station at Vecquemont (between Amiens and Peronne) for an unspecified injury or illness. It cannot have been too bad as he rejoined his regiment just three days later.

The ten-week long Arras Offensive was launched in support of a larger French offensive. The opening actions were very encouraging but the British offensive soon bogs down into the usual attritional slog and heavy casualties ensue. The 9th Gordon Highlanders were not involved in the first action (Battle of Vimy), but took part in the second, known as the first Battle of The Scarpe, which started on the day after Edward's death.

The war diary is not particularly communicative, but we know that in the week prior to Edward's death, the battalion had been hard at work preparing new and improving trenches in readiness for the attack.

In particular they had extended and deepened the communications trench, dug out and camouflaged the assembly trenches and boarded and otherwise improved several other trenches. However, the diary states that the battalion rested on April 8th.

An appendix is attached to the diary noting numbers of men joining and leaving the battalion for a multitude of reasons. Included is the column for men killed with the figure '1' inserted for April 8th – the day Edward was killed. This '1' must be Edward. But, how did he die if the battalion was not in action and was 'resting'? It is probable that Edward was either killed accidentally, or killed by a sniper or shell burst. The former would have led to a Court of Enquiry so is unlikely as there is no mention of such an enquiry in his service record. My inclination is that a sniper killed Edward.

The sum of £17 11s 6d, the sum owed to Edward at the time of his death was remitted to the Revd. Lazenby in June 1917, but sadly, the vicar, his adopted father, died on December 13th 1917 causing some confusion in the Army bureaucracy, as they didn't know who to send Edward's medals and scroll to.

Eventually they wrote to the Chief Constable of the Lincolnshire Constabulary to see if they cold find whom to contact. A Superintendent Frederick Theaker replied giving the name and address of the vicar's executor, a Maurice H Footman, solicitor of Silver Street, Lincoln.

By now it was 1919 and Mr Footman got in touch, mentioning that Edward's father in Webb Street had asked for the medals to be sent to him. That was not good enough for the Army as they had to follow the legal procedures, and so the medals were sent to Mr Footman in 1920 for distribution according to the will of the Revd. Lazenby. Whether they ended up with his proper family, we'll never know.

Edward is buried in the Faubourg D'Amiens Cemetery in Arras. The Commonwealth section of the cemetery was begun in March 1916 and continued to be used by field ambulances and fighting units until November 1918. The cemetery was enlarged after the Armistice when graves were brought in from the battlefields and from two smaller cemeteries in the vicinity.

The cemetery contains over 2,650 Commonwealth burials of the First World War, 10 of which are unidentified. Additional land was used for the construction of the Arras Memorial and Arras Flying Services Memorial, which together remember about 36,000 names.

Edward is also remembered in a special stained glass window in St Peter's Church in Torksey. The two panels show Alfred the Great and Edward the Black Prince (Alfred Lazenby and Edward Nelson) with the inscription:

Remember Alfred William Lazenby, Vicar of Torksey who died 13 December 1917 aged 59 and his adopted son, Edward William Nelson, Lce. Cpl. 3rd Battalion, Gordon Highlanders, killed in action Easter Day 1917, age 21.

The inscription has two errors of fact: his age (he was 23 when he died) and his battalion (all official records give the 9th).

WALTER BURWELL SHARPE
PRIVATE 40478, 7TH BATTALION THE NORFOLK REGIMENT
KILLED IN ACTION 24TH MARCH 1917, AGED 22

William was the eldest son of Fred Sharpe and his wife, Grace. Fred was a farm worker, employed as a waggoner and moved around a fair bit to find work. Fred had been born in Glentworth, his wife in Normanby by Spital, Walter was born in Cold Hanworth and his younger siblings in Nettleham, Glentham and Bishop Norton.

It was the in latter village that Walter had found work as in 1911 he is found as a farm labourer employed by the Willoughby family. There is a bit of a mystery as regards his parents. Grace and the children are together in Bishop Norton, but there is no sign of Fred. However, a Fred Sharpe of the right age but born in Owmby by Spital (very close to where the family had lived) is in residence at Lincoln Prison!

I have yet to find any connection between the Sharpe family and Torksey, but assume the family moved to the village some time after 1921. They were living in Sturton by Stow (not too far from Torksey) in 1939.

Walter enlisted at Lincoln into the county regiment in April 1916. His height was 5 feet 3½ inches and he weighed almost nine stone.

After training, he landed in France on September 26th 1916 and just over a fortnight later was transferred into the Norfolk Regiment. The 7th Battalion had been formed in August 1914 as part of Kitchener's First Volunteer Army and had been on the Western Front since May 1915 as part of 35th Brigade in the 12th (Eastern) Division. Walter arrived just in time for the final acts of the Battle of The Somme in which his battalion had been heavily involved and had suffered very high casualties.

The winter period was relatively quiet in terms of action. The battalion alternated between billets, and periods in the front and reserve lines with few, if any, casualties. At the beginning of March, they moved to Arras in readiness for the massive assault that would begin the following month.

On the 24th, the war diary reads:

"About 6.00am this morning the Division on our left carried out a raid whereupon the enemy retaliated by heavily shelling our Front and Support Lines, causing the following casualties: 5 killed and 6 wounded.

Some small balloons were sent over from the enemy's lines this morning. One of these came down close to Battalion HQ. It was found to have a number of papers printed in French containing propaganda against the British and evidently intended for the civil population. 'B' & 'D' Companies relieved 'A' & 'C' Companies in the Front Line. The day has been particularly quiet."

Walter was a member of 'A' Company and one of the men killed when the German shelled the Battalion's Front Line. It wasn't 'particularly quiet' for him and his comrades.

His personal effects were sent home to his parents and included his identification disc, letters and photos, a pipe, a photo case, two religious books, his soldier's pouch, a cigarette case and purse, two keys and his cap badge.

The War Office experienced some confusion as to who to send his campaign medals to. His father, Fred, was named as next of kin in his service record, but correspondence to the family home (now at 69 Bridge Street) came from his mother, Grace. A letter of explanation came from Grace in December 1919, which opens a distressing window into matters at home. It is reproduced below in its original wording:

Sir, In reply to your letter I received I am sorry to say we are only in very poor circumstances we have nothing only what we work for and my husband Frederick Sharpe is expecting getting paid off this week as they have nothing more for him to do and you asked me about y sons will no 40478 Private Walter Burwell Sharpe 7th Norfolk Regt

When he came home for is last leave he told me that he had made is will ready for going to France I was ill at the time Doctering so he did not say much as it upset me so he made is will at Weelsby Camp nr Grimsby No doubt you will be able to get a copy of it their as he went from Weelsby Camp to France

I remain Yours truly
Mrs Grace Sharpe
69 Bridge Street
Gainsborough

Monies owed to Walter amounting to £4 3s 4d were paid to his father in August 1917 but it appears the War Office couldn't find his will as there is no entry in the Probate Office records of Soldier's wills. However, his War Gratuity of £3 was paid to Fred in December 1919, and his medals followed in late 1921.

Walter is buried in the Faubourg D'Amiens Cemetery in Arras.

HARRY WARD

PRIVATE 5433, 1ST BATTALION
THE LINCOLNSHIRE REGIMENT
KILLED IN ACTION 24TH/25TH OCTOBER 1914

Whilst Harry only had a tenuous link with the parish, his parents lived there for a good portion of their lives.

Harry's parents were George and Betsy Ward and although Betsy had been born in Gainsborough, George, born in 1851, was a Brampton lad but had led quite a peripatetic life living in Bradford, Gainsborough, Scunthorpe and Burringham before returning to Brampton between 1901 and 1911.

Harry had, in fact, been born in Scunthorpe in 1882, and although his eldest child was born in Torksey in 1909, I have found no evidence to show he actually lived in the village, or, if he did, for any length of time. Equally, he has proved to be elusive in the 1901 census.

What is certain is that in 1911 he was living in South Elmsall in the West Riding of Yorkshire and working as an above ground colliery labourer. With him are his wife, Florence (born in Lincoln) and his son Frank who, as referred to above, had been born in Torksey.

Two further children were born – Phyllis in 1913 and the strangely named European Harry Ward in 1915, both born at South Elmsall.

Was Harry a reservist? His service record hasn't survived, but it would appear he arrived in France with the battalion on the afternoon of August 13th 1914 and disembarked the Union Castle liner 'Norman' at Le Havre in the early hours of the following morning.

Despite his record showing that he died in October 1914, just two months after arrival in France, his medal roll index card has no mention of the 1914 (Mons) Star he would have been eligible for.

The 1st Battalion The Lincolnshire Regiment, as part of 3rd Division, would have marched as far as the Belgian town of Mons, fighting in the Battle of Le Cateau, before retreating back to the south of the River Marne. It was here that the British Army with their French allies turned the tide of the German advance and pushed them back beyond the Marne and the Aisne before reaching the line of trenches familiar to us all now around the Belgian town of Ypres. Harry would have been involved in these actions.

What is known as the First Battle of Ypres was in reality a series of battles, some long, some short, that raged all around the Flemish town as the British fought to cling onto what became known as the Ypres Salient. The battalion were involved in the capture of the village of Herlies, and then into a series of dogged and bitter fighting to hold off the massive German attacks.

The Official History of the Lincolnshire Regiment in WW1 describes the next few days thus as it concerned the 1st Battalion:

20th October witnessed hard fighting all along the line. From Armentieres to Ypres the Germans attacked in very superior numbers, whilst south of that line British troops in the front line were called upon to beat off successive violent attacks.

The 9th Brigade, still holding the line Herlies-L'Aventure, was heavily shelled at about 9 a.m., and an hour later the German infantry advanced to the attack, but our guns caught them in the open and broke up the advance. At 12 noon another attack was launched, the Royal Fusiliers losing heavily, but the enemy made no headway and gave up the attempt at about 1.15pm.

A third attack was threatened at 2.50 p.m. against the south eastern corner of Herlies, but did not materialise. Spasmodic attempts under cover of heavy shellfire were made against the Lincolnshire line all day with no success. One shell fell in B Company's trench, killing one and wounding eight other ranks.

About 4 p.m. another shell burst over Battalion Headquarters, wounding 2nd Lieutenant Spooner, killing Pioneer-Sergeant Sole and wounding eight more men.

The 21st and 22nd were similarly days of constant action, all attacks by the enemy being repulsed with heavy losses to his infantry. On the latter date the Brigade shortened its front by withdrawing to a new line of trenches from Helpecarbe (exclusive) to Le Pluich (exclusive). The Lincolnshire therefore fell back eight hundred yards just before dawn, but were scarcely in position when the German artillery opened fire and continued to shell the position all day, killing two men and wounding nine.

On the 23rd another withdrawal took place, the 9th Brigade falling back to a line on the Richebourg-Armentieres road before daylight, the Lincolnshire

acting as rearguard. At 10am the Germans advanced and established themselves about seven hundred yards in front of the Brigade. Before dawn on the 24th, an attempt by the enemy to advance was repulsed by rifle fire.

As can be seen, it was a time of being constantly shelled and assailed by rifle and machine gun fire. Harry's record in the Commonwealth War Grave Commission's data has his date of death as October 24th; the Soldiers Died in the Great War has the 25th. What does the battalion's war diary have to say?

24th October:
The enemy attacked about 12.30am, heavy firing was kept up for about 2 hours. The enemy were repulsed. Orders were received for the Battalion to be relieved at dusk, but owing to the enemy attacking heavily on the Right of out line, this operation was unable to be carried out, the relieving Battalion having been sent in support.

25th October:
About 3.30am, the Germans again attacked but without success. Attacks continued throughout the day, a heavy rifle and machine gun fire being poured on our trenches. Casualties: two officers killed, other ranks: 9 killed, 12 wounded. Weather very wet.

The Commonwealth War Grave Commission database shows only Harry's death on the 24th, whilst eleven men from the 1st Battalion have the 25th as their date of death. Presumably, three of the wounded did not survive their wounds for long. It suggests that Harry died during the night of 24th/25th October and different records have taken one or other of the dates.

Of the twelve men killed, two are buried in Bethune Town Cemetery, whilst the bodies of the rest (including Harry) were subsequently never found or identified. Their names are among over 13,400 names inscribed on the Le Touret Memorial situated between Bethune and Armentieres.

Lincoln Golf Club Early History

In 1891, a small group of Lincoln's leading citizens made their way to the offices of Danby's solicitors, near the Stonebow in Lincoln, for what was, for them, a most important meeting. To agree to form the Lincoln Golf Club.

During the late 19th century the popularity of the game of golf in England had been expanding enormously.

Some of Lincoln's successful businessmen and professionals were determined that the city would be not be left behind. Golf was already being played in Grantham and Stamford.

Those present at the meeting in Lincoln included Waldo Sibthorp, the squire of Canwick, Leslie Melville, Robert Swan, Rev W Usher and Alfred Shuttleworth, proprietor of Clayton & Shuttleworth,

The original clubhouse in Torksey with a young golfer about to tee off! The course is part located in Torksey and part located in Brampton

a major agricultural equipment manufacturer. This firm went on to produce several thousand aeroplanes during the First World War. Alfred Shuttleworth was elected President, Leslie Melville Chairman and W B Danby as temporary Secretary. It is pleasing to note that 125 years later, Torksey members are still playing for the Sibthorp Salvers and the Shuttleworth Cup.

The committee agreed to form Lincoln Golf Club and to lease an area of land adjacent to the Carholme Race Course on the West Common. An annual rental of £100 was agreed and Willie Park, a leading professional champion golfer from Musselburgh, was appointed to lay out the course.

Amazingly only some three weeks after the meeting, the nine-hole golf course was opened for play on 7th March 1891. It must have been extremely basic with the nine holes being cut into the turf, a little bit of tidying up and that was that!

An early meeting resolved that, on major social occasions, the uniform of the club was to be a red coat with a Lincoln green collar, and brass buttons engraved with the words Lincoln Golf Club 1891. Mr Captain, I think you would look incredibly smart in such an outfit today! A ladies' section was formed around 1895 at a special subscription rate.

The first members had a frustrating time as the course was on common land, which meant that animals were grazing on the course, and this resulted in much offensive matter on the fairways! The fact that the public also had access to the ground didn't help matters.

Archie Earl, the Club's first professional player

However they soldiered on but were not encouraged by the establishment of an isolation camp for smallpox patients. There was a serious epidemic at the time. The camp was set up on the West Common, very near to the course, and this worried club members considerably.

A subcommittee of members was hastily formed and asked to seek out more suitable land near Lincoln. They looked at areas around Hykeham and also Torksey. They went by train from Lincoln Central to Torksey - older members will remember the railway station just

147

to the left of the 15th fairway. They liked the look of this land and in July 1903 they recommended to the committee that 57 acres, sufficient for a long nine-hole course, had been located at Torksey, with turf of a fine seaside character over undulating natural golfing country.

An estimate was produced that the cost of a first rate nine-hole course and the building of a clubhouse at Torksey would be some £1,200, around £100,000 at today's prices. The President, Alfred Shuttleworth, promised to fund half the cost, and members, quite rightly, snapped his hand off and fully supported the recommendation.

So in 1903 J H Taylor, a top professional who had won the Open Championship several times, was invited to produce a report on the Torksey land. He said, quote, "The ground at Torksey I consider to be eminently adapted for the game. The club is to be congratulated on acquiring such a tract of land, as it is the kind of ground that one usually identifies with the best of seaside course". Archie Earl, who was the groundsman on the West Common course, was asked to prepare the new course. He later became the club's first professional and I (that is Paul) was lucky enough to have golf lessons from him in the 1950s.

Excellent progress was made, and by January 1904 the first completed holes were open for play. These were the 1st, today's 10th, 9th today's 18th, 7th today's 16th and 6th today's 15th.

The clubhouse after additional work was carried out

Golf Club House, Torksey. 58. "The Dennis Series."

The Island Inn

LINCOLNSHIRE ECHO
SATURDAY, JANUARY 21ST 1939

"ISLAND" INN AT TORKSEY

INN SURROUNDED BY WATER
MAIN ROAD SUBMERGED

Rising water threatens to cut off main road communications between Torksey and Marton on the Lincoln/Gainsborough road.

The Castle Inn at Torksey is now on an island surrounded on either side by water. To reach the front door it is necessary to pull up a car right to the doorstep, although people cycling or wearing gumboots can reach the house.

The inn has been threatened by floods since Christmas, but it is only in the last day or so that water has been standing on the road, and is now over six inches deep, and cars passing through it make a big bow wave.

BY BOAT ACROSS FIELDS
Mr Tom Denby, the licensee, told an Echo reporter today that two of his customers last night travelled from Torksey Lock across the fields in a boat to the inn.

He added that the water in the Trent at Marton was still very high and until it went down there would be no improvement in the floods. The water is still rising steadily, and if the rain of this morning continued there was a possibility that the flooding would become worse.

Mr Denby said that the water was three or four inches

deep in his cellar and thought that it would be at least a week before the water got away,

THREAT TO ROAD TRAFFIC
Parts of Torksey Golf Course are still under water and play is impossible on several greens, although the clubhouse could still be reached without difficulty this morning. Between Marton and Torksey, near the drain which runs under the main road, water covered the road for a distance of 40 yards and the depth of the water in some places in that stretch was between six inches and a foot.

Notices warning motorists of flooding were posted at each of the stretch and an RAC guide was on duty there.

"ISLAND" INN AT TORKSEY

A motorist negotiating the flooded roadway outside the Castle Inn at Torksey, which has been completely surrounded by water for two days.

The Village Shop

Torksey shop played a big part in our lives. You could buy most everyday things there from candles to pencils and even Huntley and Palmer's fruit slab cake sold by the pound, although that was rationed so you would have to use some of your ration book points.

Miss Florrie Matthews served in the shop – possibly she was Arthur's sister and, sometimes, Miss Turnbull would be there. Perhaps she was an aunt. There was a connection to the railway station as well as they were also coal merchants.

In White's Directory of 1872 there was a Robert Turnbull who was Stationmaster, but by the 1901 edition of Kelly's Directory he was a grocer, draper and agent for the Midland Counties Insurance Company. Robert is not mentioned in Kelly's 1915 edition, but Turnbull and Matthews are listed as shopkeepers as they were in 1935.

Torksey Railway Station

By July 1849, the Manchester, Sheffield and Lincolnshire Railway (MS&L) had opened their route between Retford and Gainsborough, but were keen to get access from the south/west to Lincoln.

After the Great Northern Railway (GNR) opened their route between Lincoln and Gainsborough, the MS&L saw their opportunity and quickly obtained agreement to open a new line from Clarborough Junction on the Retford-Gainsborough line to Sykes Junction (just north of Saxilby), where it joined the GNR's Lincoln-Gainsborough route. They enjoyed running rights over the GNR's metals into Lincoln.

The line opened throughout on August 7th 1850 (they got infrastructure projects completed quickly in those days!) with three intermediate stations, two on the Nottinghamshire side at Leverington and Cottam, with Torksey on the Lincolnshire side of the River Trent.

A view of the platform at Torksey - this was probably taken shortly before the closure of the line

The line possessed one major structure - the 320 feet long Torksey Viaduct across the Trent. A steel girder bridge with massive stone abutments on either side of it had a single central pier in the river. On the Torksey side a long steel trestle-type viaduct crossed the floodplain of the river, itself over 520 feet long. The viaduct was designed by John Fowler, who later went on to design the Forth Rail Bridge.

A further view of the station and platform - all of which no longer exists

As far as Torksey Station is concerned, the buildings were demolished in 1967 and there is little left to show that a railway ran through here apart from the raised track-bed running behind the houses on the south side of Station Road. Brick abutments also survive of the girder bridges that would have carried the line over a small stream opposite the Castle Inn and the main A156 road.

In terms of staffing, the station would have had the usual complement of clerks, ticket collectors, signalmen, porters, platelayers and crossing keepers all in the charge of the 'Stationmaster'.

Judging by the number of railwaymen in Torksey, Brampton and Hardwick in the 1851 census, the station was not long established with just the Stationmaster, William Purvis (born Stow, c1823) shown as having a 'station' function.

Other railwaymen consisted of four labourers, two of whom occupied crossing keepers' cottages. No doubt their wives looked after the gates. The labourers were, presumably, platelayers looking after the trackwork.

By 1901, however, numbers had risen to fourteen railway-associated individuals:

TORKSEY

Stationmaster	Samuel Booth
Signalmen	John H Frow*
	William Matthews
Porter	Alfred H Frow
Foreman Platelayer	Thomas F Bourn

Platelayers	John Smith
	John W Robinson
	Thomas Hunter

HARDWICK

Signalmen	Edwin N Jeans
	John Way
Signalman Learner	Joseph E Jeans
Platelayers	William Emmingham
	Joseph Hardy

BRAMPTON

Signalman	Fred Jackson

One of John Frow's sons was killed in the First World War at Arras in April 1917 whilst serving with the 5th Battalion The Yorkshire Regiment.

The apparent lack of crossing keepers is probably due to the fact that individual residences were rarely named in the 1901 census whilst being shown in the 1851 census. Probably some of the platelayers lived at the crossings and again their wives fulfilled the

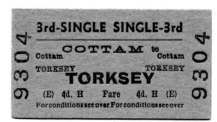

A selection of the paper train tickets that would have been issued from Torksey Station

crossing duties.

By the end of October 1939 the numbers had dropped commensurate with the fall in traffic levels:

NAME	POSITION	WAGE
Maurice Charles Kew*	Porter/Signalman	£2 6s 6d p/w
Eric Jackson Backhouse*	Porter	£2 5s 0d p/w
Louisa Kew*	Crossing Keeper	£1 18s 0d p/w
Rose Hurst	Gatewoman	£0 1s 6d p/w

The staff marked * had a small rent deduction made from their wages for living in railway-owned accommodation.

The bridge that crossed the road to take trains over the river Trent has since been removed

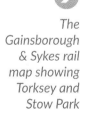

One of the original signal boxes at Torksey Station

As late as 1938 there were quite a few trains in both directions with most stopping at Torksey. Additionally there were excursion trains from Yorkshire to the Lincolnshire coast and fishermen's specials taking anglers from places like Sheffield and Rotherham through Torksey and Lincoln to the Lincolnshire Loop Line between Lincoln and Boston, which closely followed the River Witham throughout its length.

However, post-war traffic levels dropped considerably and the line closed in late 1959. A late flowering of traffic occurred after an oil depot opened at Torksey during the Second World War. Deliveries were made by river to begin with, but from 1966 two sidings were laid just before the viaduct with the section from Sykes Junction to the depot being operated as a private siding.

Daily traffic from Ellesmere Port continued until the depot closed in 1988 and, soon after, the bridge carrying the line over the Lincoln to Gainsborough main road at the northern end of Torksey was removed, presumably on the grounds of saving maintenance costs.

A section of line remains in place on the Nottinghamshire side to serve new sidings accommodating 'merry-go-round' trains from the Nottinghamshire coalfield to Cottam Power Station. Coal is now mainly imported from abroad.

The Gainsborough & Sykes rail map showing Torksey and Stow Park

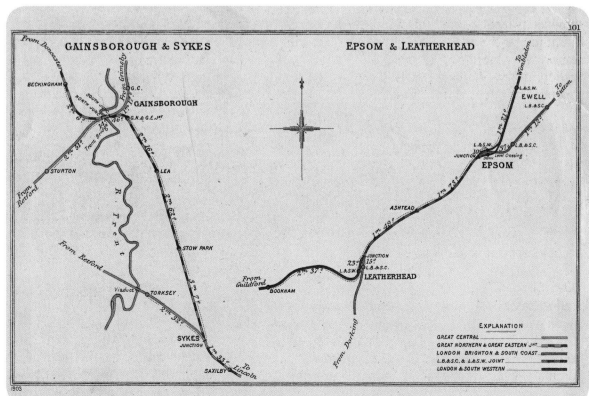

Torksey, the Town that Died

Torksey has a very chequered history. Inhabited first by the ancient Celtic tribes along the Trent valley, then civilised and extended by the Romans and favoured by the Danes, its fortunes rose and fell with the times.

It was probably the Romans who saw the possibilities of linking the Trent to their town at Lincoln. The Anglo Saxons who followed gave the town the name Tiovulfingacester and built a grain warehouse and a mound to secure the navigation, believed to have been on the north side of the present day lock.

It was the canal and river that made Torksey important. Kings, bishops and other important churchmen and their messengers were conveyed between Lincoln and York, the local burgesses supplying them with provisions. In his history, the Venerable Bede said "An old man of utmost veracity," told he was baptised "with a great multitude by Bishop Paulinus in the presence of King Edwin (Saxon King of Northumbria) near the city of Tiovulfingacester".

In 873 AD, the Danes came to Lindsey and "Wintered there at a place called Turcesige" a name preferred by the later Saxons. Later when Sweyn Forkbeard entered England by the Humber, he is said to have dominated Lincoln and Torksey from his base at Gainsborough. If that seems a little far-fetched today, it should be noted that the Domesday Book placed Torksey as a borough next after Lincoln and Stamford.

An early view of the main road, Torksey

The rot had set in before Domesday however. As the canal silted up and lost both its importance and its wealthy and distinguished travellers, the town slowly began to die. Taxes went up and the population dispersed. Never did they fall further that when the burgesses reportedly chose to oppose the Norman Conquest.

There were brief spells of renown. During the period known as the Anarchy (covering the civil war between supporters of the Empress Matilda, and King Stephen who had seized the throne), Ranulph, Earl of Chester, a supporter of Matilda, eager to relieve the forces besieged in Lincoln Castle by the King in 1141, swam across the flooded Trent at Torksey with horses and baggage as the ferry was too slow!

Later, the man who would be Henry the Second conferred the Lordship of Torksey on Ranulph for helping his mother, Matilda, and the King granted a charter to Torksey confirming a market and free customs.

The first religious house in Torksey was licensed by King John in about 1200. It stood at the northern edge of the town, near the present church of St Peter. Townspeople themselves founded a small Cistercian priory inhabited by nuns on the south side of the Fossdyke. It was sensibly dedicated to St Nicholas, the patron saint of sailors. However, due to favour and support being lost, both these establishments remained poor to the last.

One piece of history has been saved. The altar stone of St Peter's is also the sepulchral slab of Margaret de Multon, the last Abbess of St Nicholas. Of the three churches known to have been built in the parish of Torksey, little is known except for the surviving St Peter's in the present village centre. Its oldest feature is now the Transitional Norman font, if you discount the small pre-Christian effigy worshipped by the early Britons, high on the south wall and found within nearby ruins many years ago.

There is also a beautiful window showing the Crucifixion and Ascension, a gift of the Cust family, former Lords of the Manor. The well-cared-for church can be visited by arrangement with the churchwardens.

One showpiece that many larger villages cannot boast is the castle, east of the houses nearest the Trent. The ruin is still imposing but its history belies its looks.

It was built in 1560 by the Jermyn family and later passed to the Dukes of Newcastle and then back again. It had little strength as a fortress since there were no ditches or other outworks and, after bombardment by civil war troops on their way to Newark by river, it was never rebuilt. It remains a

The Castle, Torksey   40.   "The Dennis Series"

An early photograph of Torksey Castle from The Dennis Series

This image shows the west view of Torksey Castle (called here Torksey Hall). The image was created by S Buck in 1726 and is signed 'His most obedient humble servant'.

picturesque ruin, washed in hard winters by the flooded Trent and becoming the temporary stately home of a kestrel family in spring.

The old castle is best seen from a public footpath going north from Torksey, to the east of the old railway bridge over the main road. At the top of a slight rise there is an old railway viaduct bringing walkers their first views of the castle. This listed viaduct has been purchased by Sustrans who have rebuilt a crossing of the river for cyclists, walkers and horses (even wheelchairs).

The only other path to the castle is from the village through a field on private property, but a back view of it can be had from the main street.

A whole series of coins dating from the Roman occupation have been discovered, and in the British Museum a bronze statuette of Mars has been preserved, found in the Fossdyke in 1773. It bears the singular inscription 'For 100 Sesterces, Celatus the coppersmith made this figure and delivered the

The West View of Torksey Hall near Gainsborough in the County of Lincoln

pound of copper when wrought for three denarii'.

Skipping over a few centuries of slow decline, there was once a railway passing east to west through the present village. It left the Lincoln to Gainsborough line at Sykes Junction, had a station in Torksey, passed over the Trent viaduct and made for Retford. There is little trace of the line visible today, but a few remains can be found. The stones from the station were removed some years ago and reused elsewhere in the village.

There are still a few people who remember how everyone set their watches by the shrill whistle of the train each day at noon. It bustled importantly across the Trent bound for Retford and Sheffield.

Today, the A156 between Torksey Lock and the village passes fields where, under the ground now, the main town lay. Two abbeys and two of the three churches remain only as brief mentions in books. We do not even know what they looked like. Strangely, it was recorded that when an elm tree struggled to grow in the ruins of one, the villagers took away the walls to spare the tree, using the stone for roads.

Bridge over Trent, Torksey. no 43.   "The Dennis Series"

Torksey Viaduct which today has been converted to a public walking path by Sustrans

There have been a number of archaeological digs carried out in and around the village and the ground gives up tantalising glimpses of what were quite busy and densely packed lives. Skeletons have been unearthed as well as many interesting artefacts.

Today, the village is without a shop or school. Hardly an original Torkseyite remains. The common land is now a golf course. It has lost its one fast beating heart to the whims of time and the dictates of modern rural decay.

Even so, just occasionally, when the moon glows through thin clouds and is reflected in the lazy river, the ghosts of centuries can appear to rise in the mist from their hiding places to remind the imaginative watcher of Torksey's place in history.

The Rose Family of Torksey

As is our wont, non-farming people are more likely to conjure up a romantic picture of farming in the past of horse-drawn wagons moving across straw-strewn fields and muscled horses pulling ploughs through rich, dark soil. But in reality, in years gone by the work was hard, cold and dirty and overall it meant long hours of toil.

The picture is now further removed with the modern reality of heavy machinery carrying out the jobs in a fraction of the time, which an army of workers would have needed days to complete.

A top-of-the-range combine harvester can achieve in a few dusty and noisy hours what a small army of agricultural labourers would have taken days and weeks to carry out a hundred years ago.

However, we are not only talking as far back as Victorian or Edwardian times. Mechanisation really began to take off in the decades immediately after the Second World War, with high-tech farming encroaching on this apparent 'utopia' in the late 1960s and early 1970s.

Henry Ford first introduced the Fordson tractor, a model more affordable than previous models, in the years around the First World War with production starting in England in the 1920s. These early models brought affordable mechanisation to many farmers and kick-started the revolutionary change in farming.

Also, by 1950, there were around 15,000 combine harvesters in the UK. These were expensive and not every farm had one, with some farms still keeping the feel of a technology-free environment.

There are numerous local farming families who have experienced the huge change as described within our own area, but this short story concentrates on the Rose family of Torksey:

 Photograph taken at Stow Park Farm in c.1922 Family members: L-R back row - Ernest, Annie, William, Edith, Ethel. L-R mid row - Agnes, George, Emma, Albert. L-R front row - Walter Richard.

George Rose is a prime example of 'climbing the ladder of hard work' as he began his working life as an agricultural labourer, rising up the ladder to wagoner, farm bailiff, tenant farmer and finally to farm owner. George and his family moved to Highwood Farm around 1929, the family having being involved with a few farms before then.

George's parents, John and Esme Rose, came from Bishop Norton and John is buried in the graveyard there together with his parents, Elizabeth and William Rose. George was born at Thonock near Gainsborough, opposite Williamson's Farm, and when he was older he worked at White House Farm, which is near the Morrison's supermarket in Gainsborough.

George had five sons and four daughters. Walter Wheatley Rose (known as Wally) was the fourth son and it is Wally's farming life that we shall follow.

When Wally was about five or six in 1922, his father George was made Bailiff of the Co-op farm at Stow Park that is now owned by H Barker and Sons.

William Langley had previously been the tenant of Highwood Farm, just across the road from Stow Park Farm, and entries in the farm ledgers now belonging to the Rose family give a snapshot of life on the farm in the early 1930s:

1929 – November 5th Couple of rabbits sold at 2s 6d (12.5p) 'a couple' at Stennett's Auction in Gainsborough

1930 – Horse bought – 16-years-old for £17 6s 6d (£17.32). Coal bought – 1 ton 3 cwt. for £1 5s 3d (£1.26)

1931 – Two carts repaired by Wardell, Sturton by Stow for £3 15s 4d (£3.76). Wages for two men for 2 days work – 19s (9s 6d each for two days).

These costs in the old currency appear amazing but at the time it was hard to make a living as the country was in the grip of the Great Depression (1929-1932). This came at a time when the United Kingdom was still recovering from the effects of the First World War. It was a period of national economic downturn and British farming was in trouble.

The prices of farm produce had collapsed, land was going out of cultivation, the numbers employed in agriculture were declining and many farmers faced bankruptcy. In this climate it was a matter of survival for all families and those farmers who did survive were those who were self-sufficient – keeping pigs and selling off small quantities of their larger livestock locally.

The move to Highwood Farm was the last and this was where the family finally put down roots and Wally lived out his working life here. He married Grace Cox in 1945 and they had two sons and one daughter – Derek, Ivan and Jean. Sadly Ivan died aged 14 in 1962.

Grace had been born on June 1st 1920 in Londonthorpe near Grantham, the eldest of five. She went into service at the age of 14 and moved to Coleby to a family called Mason who farmed at The Laurels. Her family moved to Torksey in 1933 when her father went to work for Mr William Gourley at Firs Farm, a job that he kept for the next thirty-five years.

When war broke out in 1939 Grace had to register and had the choice of the armed forces or factory work. She chose to work at Rose Brothers in Gainsborough (no relation to her husband's family) and worked there for four years. It was hard work, rising early to leave home at 5.15am and cycle to Gainsborough from Torksey ready to start her shift

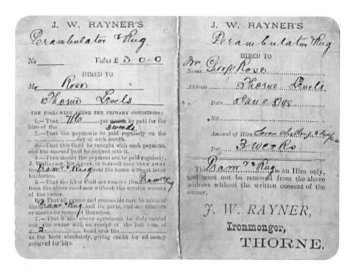

A scanned copy of a hire purchase card in the name of Mr George Rose dated 1898. Taken out for the purchase of a perambulator and rug to the total value of £3 through J W Rayner, Ironmonger, Thorne, near Doncaster. The words 'RAYNER'S CYCLE WORKS' can still be read on the roof slates of the building which housed J W Rayner in Thorne, but at some time between 1904 and 1908 the name above the door was replaced by that of John William Hirst. Hirst's ironmonger's was legendary in Thorne and beyond, comparable to an Aladdin's cave in the range of goods on sale but the business is no longer there.

at 6.00am. She would leave for home at 5.00pm in the evening. For the last ten months of her factory life, Grace took lodgings in Gainsborough as the long hours and cycling backwards and forwards in all weathers were beginning to take their toll.

In 1945 she was released from factory work to marry Wally and the wedding was held on May 19th in Torksey. Her landlady made the wedding cake and helped organise the celebrations.

Families were close and lived and worked together to ensure success and the Rose family were no exception. Life continued and slowly the world began to intrude on lives at Highwood Farm.

A telephone was installed in January 1934 at a total cost of £2 2s 2d (£2 12p) made up as follows:

Hand phone	£0 5s 0d
Connection	£0 15s 0d
Rent	£1 2s 2d

The ledgers show the average cost of monthly calls was just over £1 4s 0d (£1.20).

The war still had an input and land girls were still being employed on the farm in 1947 as an entry in the ledgers for that year show:

3 Land Girls for 2 days threshing - £3 10s 5d (£3.52)

Local businesses were always on hand too:

2 days threshing by Davey – cost £10 15s (£10.75)

This would be Herbert Davey of Sturton by Stow whose descendants still live in Sturton.

Prisoners of war were also used on the farm until the late 1940s and as mentioned in the September 2013 edition of Trentside Links, a lot of these 'prisoners' never went home but stayed and made their new home in the United Kingdom.

Matters started to look up as in 1947 there is an entry in the ledgers for the purchase of a new Fordson Major Tractor at a cost of £304 15s 9d (£304.78).

The following decades passed at Highwood Farm with all the usual stories and events which make up family life. Wally ran the farm and Grace ran the family making sure everyone did their duty to help each other.

Bringing the date up the 1980s and 1990s, the family were still very self-reliant and two of Wally's brothers, Ernie and Dick who also lived and worked on the farm, were more than happy to stay within the farm confines and not even bother to travel as far as Lincoln. The farm and their family were sufficient for their needs.

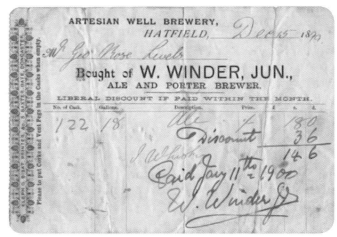

A brewery docket for 18 gallons of ale from the Artesian Well Brewery, Hatfield near Doncaster for 18s with a discount of 3s 6d, totalling 14s 6d bought by Mr George Rose and paid in full on January 11th 1900. Bearing in mind that this works out at today's prices at less than 1p per pint!

Wally died in 2010 aged 94 and Grace died in 2011 aged 90, not long after she spoke to Roger Brownlow about her life at Highwood Farm. Highwood is now farmed by Derek Rose and we are grateful to him for the loan of his grandfather's account book and photographs, and for the information in this article. Steven is the heir apparent and he is keen to keep the family tradition going into the future.

MY STORY

Margaret Scott

Margaret Lock as she then was, moved to Torksey with her family when she was fourteen years old. She was one of eight children having four brothers and three sisters. She had also just left school.

The family lived in the white house, opposite The Hume Arms. The white house was pulled down some years ago and a bungalow built in its place. During the English Civil War, the house was used as stables and there were still rings in the skirting board where the horses used to be tied up. The family presumed the soldiers lived upstairs above the stables.

An early picture of Torksey (date unknown) showing the white house opposite The Hume Arms

There were three bedrooms and a box room in the house. One Christmas, Margaret and her sister were sleeping in the box room as relatives came to stay. They slept with the box room door open, as there was no window in the room. Margaret's sister woke up and saw a figure of a soldier leaning over Margaret. He was wearing a breastplate and a metal hat like ones the Cavaliers used to wear, but her sister didn't tell Margaret until twenty years later when they were no longer living there.

The school was opposite. It could be hired privately by the village and was cleared for dances, wedding receptions and other events. The youth club met there and they put on a show each year for the villagers with singing, dancing and plays. The club was run by Mr Walter Weaver and Mr & Mrs Barraclough.

The village shop was round the corner. It was a grocer's, drapers and hardware store all rolled into one. Margaret bought her 'bottom drawer' from there including a dinner service, blankets, sheets and pillowcases. It was all in the 'utility' style as this was during the 1950s and rationing and coupons still remained from the Second World War.

A Mr Frow lived in the three-storey house. He went on his bicycle around all the

An aerial view of Torksey showing the castle and the site of the original caravan park

villages collecting the rates. There was a row of cottages and a chapel at the back of the church and they used to attend special services there.

Margaret worked at Blakey's oatmeal factory in Lincoln until her mother became ill and she had to look after her and do the housework. Later when she was nineteen, Margaret went to work at Rose's in Saxilby. She was picked up and brought home again after work, so no cycling in all weathers and no waiting for the bus!

Margaret left Torksey on her marriage in 1963 to Ken Scott and moved a few miles up the A156 to Marton where she has remained, though not in the same house.

Shirley Bury

Memories of Torksey keep cropping up. I my jottings unless they are libellous.

When I was young Newton hardly registered with me. Not many cars and very few phones. We had Mrs Barrowcliff at the Post Office and Mrs Hughes in Brampton to keep us up-to-date with local issues. Mrs B would tell my folks that "We lived down a drive till you know nowt".

Another link was the school and the canal. Miss Talbot was the head teacher in the Big Room, a fiery don't know how interesting they are to the present residents. I am 76 this week and feeling 'venerable' but do publish little woman who scared me. Sometimes she went up to the canal side

to persuade the families living on the barges that the children should be in school, so we would have a group of five or six kids to swell the register. They would stay a few days just about long enough to write their names in an exercise book and then they'd disappear back to Hull.

I particularly re-call The Elms when my parents lived there (1947-1959). There was also an over-60s party at Marton, Mr Carotte who kept Marton shop would attend along with my parents Percy and Queenie Bradbury.

They bought Mr Glen's bungalow in Marton when he bought The Elms, so they swapped houses and I believe 'flitting' day was a nightmare!

TORKSEY IN PICTURES

A picture from one of the archaeological digs undertaken in Torksey

A picture of the original Elm House taken in 1947

Torksey Ned - A local character who lived on the banks of the River Trent

A postcard from Torksey also showing the Lock area

A picture of the pupils at Torksey School in 1938/39

The original school at Torksey prior to its closure and conversion

The old school building underwent a further conversion to a family home now known as L'Ecole

A postcard from Torksey from sometime in the 1970s

An early picture of The Hume Arms

A picture of the original Torksey Post Office

A picture of children standing in the street in Torksey in approximately 1900

An aerial view of Torksey taken in approx 1989 which still shows the rail bridge in place and the site of the original caravan park.

Torksey choir at the vicarage garden party in approximately 1961

Elm House was converted to act as a property and shop, today it is being rebuilt as a family home

Once closed the school went through its conversion to a private dwelling

Torksey School pupils in approximately 1965

Floods at Torksey in 1932 with Torksey Castle shown in the background

TORKSEY LOCK

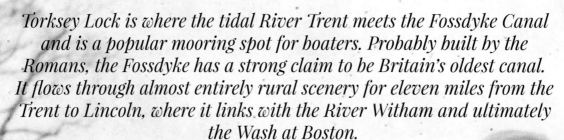

Torksey Lock is where the tidal River Trent meets the Fossdyke Canal and is a popular mooring spot for boaters. Probably built by the Romans, the Fossdyke has a strong claim to be Britain's oldest canal. It flows through almost entirely rural scenery for eleven miles from the Trent to Lincoln, where it links with the River Witham and ultimately the Wash at Boston.

A group of residents skating on the frozen water at Torksey Lock

VILLAGE TALES

The Waters of Time

Take a few minutes to travel back in time – about 2000 years. The Romans were at Torksey Lock, building the Fossdyke Canal, which is probably Britain's oldest man-made waterway. Why did they build it?

A barge passing through the lock with a young child stood on top. Some of the old houses and buildings that no longer exist can be seen on the left

The most likely reason was for transporting goods such as salted lamb to Lincoln. Imagine doing all that work without the aid of diggers and dumper trucks! After the Romans left, the Fossdyke slowly silted up until, in 1121, Henry the First ordered the canal to be

cleaned out and made good – was this Britain's first canal restoration?

The fortunes of the canal went up and down for several hundred years. In 1620, after nearly 500 years of Royal ownership and neglect, James I gave the canal to Lincoln City Council and relieved the Crown of a huge financial liability.

In 1671 another big maintenance programme was carried out by just sixty years later, the waterway was almost impassable again.

In extreme weather the Fossdyke would freeze over and residents would venture onto the ice!

In 1741, a Sheffield banker, Richard Ellison, leased the canal from the council and spent three years restoring it. The canal was back in business, mainly carrying agricultural produce from Lincolnshire to the Midlands and beyond.

The arrival of steam-powered boats in 1817 saw the first serious passenger transport on the canal. Cargo and passenger boats did quite a good trade for a few years, but the canal was again being neglected and it sometimes flooded after heavy rain. There is one story of a steam packet being carried off into the neighbouring countryside during a flood!

The fortunes of the canal continued reasonably

well until the railways arrived. The Great Northern Railway took over the lease of the Fossdyke while it built the railway alongside it for some distance. Once the railway was complete, the waterway carried less and less.

Today, people use the navigation mainly for pleasure, enjoying the freedom of the waterways and the wildlife they support.

 An example of some of the machinery and working boats that would have been found at Torksey Lock

A VIP Visit to Torksey Lock

In the spring of 1833, the then proprietors of the Fossdyke Canal asked a very famous and, arguably, our greatest engineer to do a survey of their canal. This was Isambard Kingdom Brunel and the reason for the request was criticism levelled at the owners by the boat owners. Brunel travelled to Lincoln and set to work on the project.

He travelled by packet boat up the canal to the Trent Lock at Torksey and then from Lincoln down the Witham, taking soundings from which he prepared cross-sections of the channel.

He then took a loaded boat from Torksey drawn by two horses and had little difficulty until he entered the River Witham. The keel of the boat stuck fast at High Bridge and the boat then had to be dragged through with a windlass.

After a stay of four days, Brunel returned to London, but not until after he had looked at the 'exceedingly beautiful' cathedral.

Two weeks later he came back to Lincoln to deliver his report and then went on to Boston to see Boston Stump and called it "The most complete and beautiful thing I have ever seen".

 Isambard Kingdom Brunel. Perhaps our greatest engineer

MY STORY

Terry & Kenneth Worrall

My brother and I spent much of our childhood in our caravan at Rydal Mount (now Torksey Caravan Park) because of the bombing where we lived in South Yorkshire. These are a few of my memories of those times.

I have always been interested in airfields and aircraft, hence my recollections. On one occasion I was with my parents who were talking to Maurice Ward, the owner of the caravan site, in June 1940 when a Hampden bomber came over the caravans flying at a height of about 20 feet. The bomber hit the power lines that are near the first clapper gate on the Trent Arm.

The bomber (number P4337 from 61 Squadron) carried on flying and landed back at Scampton and was declared a write-off! There is still a pole and high tension wires on the same spot.

The army had soldiers living in tents on the Trent Arm where horses now graze but it was busy in 1940-1941. At times I used to go in the boats they had.

On one occasion the soldiers were drilling holes about four inches in diameter on the bridge by the lock. I asked one soldier what they were for and he said they filled them with tar. If the Germans came they could get the tar out quickly and put dynamite in the holes and blow the bridge up to slow the enemy down.

From 1940 there used to be convoys of army lorries, Bren-Gun carriers and despatch riders on their motorcycles. They usually stopped by the White Swan at Torksey Lock because, at that time, it was like a large layby. I usually went to talk to the soldiers as from the caravan site I could see convoys approaching from Fenton.

My brother Kenneth went to Torksey School (he is three years older that I am). In the Trentside Links issue number 166 there is a photograph of a group of children at the school in 1938 or 1939 and a pupil named Charles Spendlow is on the picture. He was a friend of my brother.

Again, during the early days of the war, an aircraft used to come over and fly very low over a bungalow on Newark Road just past the firm that does lorry repairs now. The bungalow was called 'Kaga Wong'. It has been demolished for a few years now and there is a new building on the site today.

The aircraft that flew very low over Kaga Wong was doing this because the pilot's mother was staying at the bungalow at the time. It was an Airspeed Oxford twin-engine aircraft. Unfortunately, after a period of time it went missing.

From the start of Newark Road, during the latter stages of the war, the RAF stored bombs on the grass verges about four or five feet high as far as Laughterton.

In 1970 I got my pilot's licence and bought my own light aircraft, I spent many happy hours flying up the River Trent just to experience the same picture in my mind as the Hampden bomber pilots saw. This was very different for me from flying my model aeroplanes at Rydal Mount caravan site!

Here is an old photograph of myself (with broken arm) and my brother Kenneth taken in 1941 at the caravan site. I still have my links with Torksey as my wife and I used to visit to collect blackberries and mushrooms during our courtship and since our marriage in 1958. We now have a caravan on the same site as my parents did back in

Terry Worrall and his brother Kenneth taken in 1941

my childhood. We bought this in 1998/1999 and we still travel 320 miles from our home in Cornwall to the caravan for short breaks.

TORKSEY LOCK IN PICTURES

The junction at Torksey Lock - the road to the right is the approach from Laughterton whilst the original Little London caravan park can be seen on the top left corner of the picture

The Ferryman approaching Torksey Lock followed by a series of barges

Workers at Torksey Lock - industrial machinery can clearly be seen in the background

A boat stranded at Torksey lock, the barge is attempting to pull it down a homemade runway to refloat it

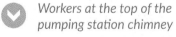

Workers at the top of the pumping station chimney

The lock and lockkeeper's house - an important connection for trade to and from Lincoln

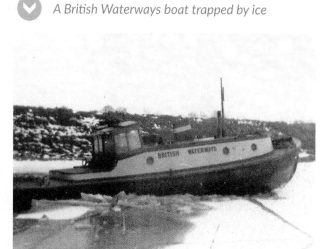

A British Waterways boat trapped by ice

Local residents at the side on the Fossdyke working on the bankside

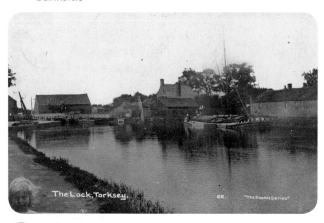

A view of the lock from the Torksey Lock bank

The pumping station located at Torksey Lock used to be steam powered and the chimney can be seen in this picture

Heavy machinery was often in use at the lock - here a crane has toppled over narrowly missing falling into the Fossdyke!

A group of workers at the suction drain at Torksey Lock

An aerial view of the lockkeeper's house, the old building to the top right has long been demolished

Sail barges would be a common site at Torksey Lock transporting goods along the water into, and from, Lincoln along the Fossdyke canal

A barge passing through the lock. This picture is more recent and shows leisure boats and caravans in the background

Residents at the house as you approach the bridge at Torksey Lock heading for Torksey

Torksey Lock was a very busy junction with access to the River Trent as you can see from this collection of barges waiting to pass through the lock